TWENTY-DOLLAR, DOLLAR, TWENTY-MINUTE™ MEALS

*for 4 people

Caroline Wright

WORKMAN PUBLISHING • NEW YORK

For my Brooklyn family

Library of Congress Cataloging-in-Publication Data is available.

ISBN 978-0-7611-7493-6

Design by Becky Terhune

Workman books are available at special discounts when purchased in bulk for premiums
and sales promotions as well as for fund-raising or educational use. Special editions or
book excerpts can also be created to specification. For details, contact the Special Sales
Director at the address below, or send an email to specialmarkets@workman.com.

Workman Publishing Company, Inc.
225 Varick Street
New York, NY 10014-4381
workman.com

WORKMAN is a registered trademark of Workman Publishing Co., Inc.

Printed in the United States of America
First printing May 2013

10 9 8 7 6 5 4 3 2 1

ACKNOWLEDGMENTS

I feel very thankful to spend my days cooking. No two days are ever alike, and they most often end at the dinner table with someone I love sharing my work. Recipes have the ability to affect a cook's life in a very real way, by turning strangers into teachers—writing recipes has certainly done that for me.

To my friends Tyler Gierber and Christiane Angeli, who believed in this project from early on and helped shape my thoughts on design and language: Thank you.

I raise a glass of local brew in thanks to the Brooklyn Kitchen for giving me a space to play and teach these recipes to eager cooks.

I am very lucky and thankful indeed to know Kylie Foxx McDonald, the editor of this book, who found a kernel of an idea in some pages I'd written and made it better than I could have ever imagined. I owe this book to you.

To my agent, Angela Miller, thank you for being my guide and for bringing such wonderful people into my life.

Thanks to my parents for giving me my first real camera and for perceiving messes in the kitchen (and every other room in their home) as a little kid's creativity.

To Jeff, Teddy, Gillian, Dan, Tyler, Claire, Neil, and Alli, who have eaten everything in this book—thanks for bringing the wine.

For Henry, who lets me use his nursery as a makeshift photo studio, thanks for arriving in our lives right on time. I can't wait to cook for you.

To my loving husband, Garth, a man of a few favorite meals that I never have the chance to cook: Thanks for everything.

CONTENTS

INTRODUCTION
ix

SALADS
2

SOUPS
23

SANDWICHES
38

PASTA
59

PIZZA
78

EGGS
93

MEAT, POULTRY + FISH
106

VEGETARIAN
143

DESSERTS
162

INDEX
185

INTRODUCTION

I lived in New York City—Brooklyn, mostly—for six years. My closest friends lived as near as the upstairs apartment in our brownstone building and only as far away as a few subway stops. Most weekends, ours was the apartment that collected all the overworked and underpaid twentysomethings who needed a good meal, though our crew of struggling actors was among the most frequent diners. I am a cook by training, profession, and nature, so I cooked for them. These friends—hungry, creative, and new to the kitchen—helped give me the confidence that the fresh and simple way I liked to create meals when alone after a long day was the way they wanted to cook, too. It is for them, and the meals we shared (more memorable than the bad movies or bottles of wine in the background), that I wrote these recipes: real food, cooked quickly and inexpensively.

Like all the meals I try to prepare, whether I'm alone or not, these recipes use simple cooking techniques, fresh produce, and ready ingredients that don't sacrifice flavor or healthfulness for time. These recipes are written to serve four people and accommodate a variety of appetites. My driving philosophy is one that is common among many of the busy cooks I know: the willingness to look at dinner differently. On some nights, dinner consists of a heaping plate of meat and vegetables, while on others it's just a simple puréed soup and a piece of crusty bread. For me, deciding what to bring to the dinner table isn't only about what is in my refrigerator; it's informed by the weather outside, what I ate that day, if I went to the gym, and if my hands are tired already. Sometimes dinner is eaten while perched on my kitchen counter before running out to a movie. Other times it's paired with dinner guests and a simple dessert that exchanges the small amount of extra time and cost, like the sweet (and quick!) recipes included here, for exponential returns in making a memorable meal. These recipes were written for all aspects of the busy life of someone who likes to eat well.

Pulling together a good, simple meal at the end of the day takes a little bit of practice and freedom to play, two skills that I encourage you to hone throughout this book. Variables such as how fast you wield a knife or how organized you are as you cook will affect the overall preparation time, especially the first time you give a dish a try. Stick with it. Also, some of the ingredients may be new to you—but I think it's part of the fun to learn to adapt a recipe to your taste, or to try out a new favorite ingredient. I hope you'll use these recipes as a guide to figuring out how you like to cook, whether by incorporating these dishes into your repertoire or by discovering elements in them that intrigue you.

I continue to learn from the pages of cookbooks, and I strongly believe in the dialogue that exists between cooks who exchange tips out of the pure love of food. I hope you'll consider this the beginning of our conversation.

An Extra Two Cents' Worth

Here are a few tips for making the most of this book:

• **GET ORGANIZED.** Read the recipes through and gather ingredients. These recipes are written to introduce the ingredients as you need them (all ingredients—except water, salt, and pepper— are highlighted), but shuffling back and forth to the refrigerator or cupboard will add to your prep time. Instead, I urge you to assemble your ingredients and tools before you start. While you're getting organized (or better yet, right when you get home), make that extra time work for you: Preheat the oven or grill, or put the pasta water on to boil.

- **CONSIDER SEASONAL SWAPS.** When debating what to make for dinner, take a good look at what's available at the market: Choose a recipe that features in-season produce, as it will be cheaper—and tastier—than out-of-season. If you have trouble finding some of the ingredients called for, try the alternatives in the margins or the variations at the bottom of the page.

- **DON'T STRESS.** Most of the time, swaps can also be made when specific oils, vinegars, butters, pasta shapes, and even types of beans are mentioned. Here are a few suggestions in case you find yourself staring at a sparse pantry:

> ✓ **Oils** I like to use mild vegetable oil, such as canola, for cooking over high heat or in dishes that have big flavors that would otherwise become muddied with a more assertive oil. However, olive oil can be used in place of almost all the oils in this book (just save the extra-virgin stuff for salads and other dishes where it won't be heated—it doesn't do well at high temperatures).

> ✓ **Vinegars** Vinegars have distinct personalities, but most often red or white wine vinegar can be used in place of anything else mentioned.

> ✓ **Butter** Salted or unsalted butter can be used interchangeably, though occasionally I'll specify one or the other. If given the luxury of choice, I prefer salted for savory dishes and unsalted for desserts.

> ✓ **Pasta** As a very general rule, I like long pastas for thick sauces, and reserve shorter pastas for light sauces thinned with pasta water. But don't let a pasta's shape stand in the way of your dinner: Most

shaped pastas that are longer than 1 inch can be used in place of long pastas.

✓ **Beans** As for beans, I choose them mostly based on texture. If you can't find the bean that's called for, pick a substitute with a similar color and/or size.

✓ **Chiles** A number of these recipes call for fresh hot chiles. I generally use a moderately spicy pepper, like jalapeño, serrano, or Fresno. If you don't have fresh peppers on hand, substitute ¼ to ½ teaspoon hot red pepper flakes for each chile listed.

• **KEEP SALAD GREENS ON HAND.** Some of these recipes are written for a lighter meal, maybe to be enjoyed after a hearty lunch or a good workout (or, in my case, after stuffing my face all day in a test kitchen somewhere). I round out a lot of meals with a simple salad of lightly dressed greens seasoned with salt and pepper. I keep salad greens on hand at all times by washing a head or two of good, crisp lettuce on the weekend (I'm partial to romaine, green leaf lettuce, and arugula), then laying out the washed leaves on a long strip of paper towels and rolling them up like a jelly roll. Stored this way in a ziplock bag, the washed greens will last up to 5 days.

To make a simple dressing, I whisk together any of a variety of vinegars or lemon juice and olive oil in a ratio of 1 part acid to 3 parts oil. Sometimes I make a lot of dressing in a leftover washed jar and store it in the refrigerator. This way, salad can be as easy as grabbing a handful of greens and giving a jar a shake.

Some Salad Dressing Favorites

- 1 tablespoon Dijon mustard + 1 tablespoon balsamic vinegar + 3 tablespoons olive oil

- 1 tablespoon chopped shallot + 1 tablespoon Sherry vinegar + 3 tablespoons walnut oil

- 1 tablespoon chopped capers + 1 tablespoon fresh lemon juice or white wine vinegar + 3 tablespoons extra-virgin olive oil

• **WORK IT.** Some of these recipes are more active than others and will keep you busy for the full twenty minutes. You may have two pots on the stove at once, or need to be chopping vegetables while something comes to a boil. Read your recipes before you begin so you know where to crank up the volume.

• **GIVE YOUR PANTRY A LITTLE LOVE.** When you cook with so few ingredients, the flavor and quality of each one makes a difference. Buy a good bottle of extra-virgin olive oil—only for those moments when a final drizzle is required—and invest in a little box of sea salt. Use a spice grinder to coarsely grind black peppercorns every few weeks and store the grounds in an airtight container. These details may cost you an occasional extra $20 bill, but will enhance the flavor (and effort) of your cooking immeasurably.

A Note on Costs

Some of these recipes call for pantry items, like spices, that can push your budget if you have to buy a brand-new bottle. While I'd prefer it if every recipe cost you $20 *or less,* I'll hope you'll think of any extra dollars spent as an investment in future meals!

Spring Green Salad with Poached Chicken + Buttermilk Dressing

Preheat the oven to 350°F.

Tear ½ medium baguette into pieces, and toss on a large rimmed baking sheet with 2 tablespoons olive oil and salt and pepper. Bake, tossing once, until the croutons are golden and crisp, about 10 minutes.

Meanwhile, simmer 2 boneless, skinless chicken breast halves (8 ounces each) in a medium skillet with 1 sliced lemon, 2 sprigs fresh rosemary, 1 small bunch fresh thyme, and enough water to barely cover, until the chicken is nearly cooked through, about 10 minutes. Let the chicken cool on a cutting board, about 8 minutes, and shred.

While the chicken cools, stir together in a small bowl ¾ cup buttermilk, 2 tablespoons sour cream, 1 tablespoon fresh thyme leaves, 1 tablespoon cider vinegar, and chopped whites of 3 scallions (slice and reserve the greens); season the dressing generously with salt and pepper. Rinse and dry 12 cups (8 ounces) salad greens.

In a large serving bowl, toss the shredded chicken with the salad greens, croutons, scallion greens, and 1 cup halved radishes. Drizzle with the dressing and serve.

Grilled Escarole with Peaches, Prosciutto, Mozzarella + Basil Oil

Preheat a grill pan over medium-high heat.

Puree ¼ cup olive oil and ½ cup fresh basil leaves in a blender until smooth; strain and set the basil oil aside.

In a large serving bowl, whisk together 1 tablespoon olive oil and 1 tablespoon balsamic vinegar; season with salt and pepper. Cut 1 small head escarole in half lengthwise and toss in the bowl with the dressing until coated.

Cook the escarole on the hot grill pan, turning once, until charred in spots, 3 to 4 minutes. Cut each section of escarole in half lengthwise again, making quarters; arrange on a platter with 2 peaches, cut into wedges; 4 ounces prosciutto (about 8 slices), torn into strips; and 1 pound fresh mozzarella, pulled into pieces.

Before serving, drizzle with the basil oil and season with salt.

ALSO TRY:
grilled endive + plums + prosciutto + mozzarella + parsley oil

Grilled Summer Squash + Haloumi Salad

A salty, semi-hard cheese with a high melting point; available at specialty food markets

Cut 1 pound haloumi cheese into ½-inch-thick slices and arrange on a plate; place in the freezer to chill. Preheat a grill pan over high heat.

Thinly slice 2 yellow summer squash into strips (about ⅛ inch thick) and place in a shallow heat-proof dish. Heat ¼ cup olive oil, 1 sliced garlic clove, 2 teaspoons finely grated lemon zest, and ¼ teaspoon red pepper flakes in a small skillet over medium heat until fragrant, about 2 minutes. Pour the hot oil mixture over the squash and toss until coated; season with salt and pepper.

Cook the squash in batches on the hot grill pan until charred and cooked through, 2 to 3 minutes per batch; set aside. Cook the haloumi on the grill pan until charred, about 2 minutes per side; set aside. Add 1 pint grape tomatoes to the grill pan and cook, tossing, until slightly softened and charred, about 2 minutes.

While the tomatoes cook, rinse and dry the leaves from 1 bunch arugula. Arrange the squash on salad plates with the arugula, tomatoes, and haloumi; season with salt and pepper. Drizzle with additional olive oil, and serve with lemon wedges.

Warm Cranberry Bean Salad with Greens + Breadcrumbs

Or black-eyed peas

Bring ½ cup olive oil, 3 cups water, 1½ cups dry white wine, 2 tablespoons grainy Dijon mustard, and 8 sprigs fresh thyme to a boil in a large skillet; add 3 cups shelled fresh cranberry beans (from about 2½ pounds pods). Season with salt and pepper. Cook, covered, over medium-high heat until the liquid has evaporated, and the beans are just tender and beginning to brown, 18 to 20 minutes.

Meanwhile, heat 2 tablespoons olive oil in a small skillet over medium heat. Add ½ cup fresh breadcrumbs and cook, tossing, until golden, 3 to 5 minutes; season with salt and pepper. While the breadcrumbs toast, rinse and dry 8 cups (about 6 ounces) baby arugula.

Transfer the hot beans to a large bowl with the arugula and toss until the greens are wilted. Serve in salad bowls, topped with the breadcrumbs. *Or baby spinach*

ALSO TRY:
dried lentils (cook about 10 minutes) + cherry tomatoes + arugula + breadcrumbs

Cold Spicy Soba + Spinach Salad with Shrimp

Bring a large saucepan of salted water to a boil over high heat.

Meanwhile, stir together in a medium bowl the sliced whites of 2 scallions (slice and reserve the greens), 1 tablespoon minced fresh ginger, 2 minced garlic cloves, 2 tablespoons vegetable oil, 2 tablespoons soy sauce, 2 to 3 teaspoons fish sauce, and 1 teaspoon Sriracha sauce; season with salt to taste.

Place 6 ounces small shrimp (such as rock or bay shrimp) in a sieve and submerge in the boiling water until cooked through, 1 to 2 minutes; set aside. Then cook 12 ounces soba noodles in the boiling water for 6 minutes.

Meanwhile, rinse the leaves from 2 bunches spinach well and tear into pieces. Add the spinach to the noodles and continue to cook until the noodles and spinach are tender, about 3 minutes. Drain and run under cold water, then press gently to remove excess liquid.

Transfer the noodles and spinach to a serving bowl, add the shrimp, and toss with the sauce, scallion greens, and 1 tablespoon sesame seeds until coated.

ALSO TRY:
soba + snow peas + skinless salmon fillet (poached about 7 minutes)

Lentil + Tuna Salad
with Kalamata Olives

Whisk together 2 tablespoons extra-virgin olive oil,
1 tablespoon fresh lemon juice, and 1 tablespoon Dijon
mustard in a medium bowl; season the dressing with
salt and pepper and set aside.

In a serving bowl, toss together 1 can (15 ounces)
lentils, rinsed and drained; 1 can (8 ounces) tuna in oil,
drained and flaked; ½ small red onion, thinly sliced;
1 cup Kalamata olives, pitted and cracked; and ½ cup
fresh parsley leaves. Season the salad with salt and
pepper, drizzle with the dressing, and serve.

Smash the olives with
the bottom of a can to
split and pit them.

Panzanella with Green Olives, Mozzarella, Prosciutto + Tomatoes

Smash the olives with the bottom of a can to split and pit them.

Tear about 10 ounces stale crusty bread (from a 6-inch loaf) into bite-size pieces.

In a large bowl, combine the bread with ⅓ cup green olives, pitted and cracked (about 8 whole olives); 8 ounces fresh mozzarella, torn into pieces; 4 ounces prosciutto, torn into pieces; 4 plum tomatoes, cut into rough chunks; 1 can (15 ounces) butter beans, rinsed and drained; and 1 tablespoon fresh oregano leaves.

Drizzle the salad with 2 tablespoons balsamic vinegar and 2 tablespoons extra-virgin olive oil, season with salt and pepper, toss, and serve.

Or cannellinis

ALSO TRY:
stale crusty bread + grilled vegetables + chickpeas + pickled cherry peppers + red wine vinegar

Zucchini Ribbon Salad with Potatoes, Ricotta Salata, Dill, Peas + Radishes

Fill a large saucepan with water to a depth of 2 inches, add salt, and bring it to a simmer over medium-low heat.

Arrange 8 small new potatoes (about 12 ounces total), halved, in a steamer basket and set the basket in the pan. Cover and steam the potatoes until tender, 10 to 12 minutes. Transfer the potatoes and 1 cup frozen peas to a colander and run under cold water until the potatoes are cool and the peas have thawed.

While the potatoes cook, use a vegetable peeler to shave 4 zucchini and/or yellow summer squash into a medium bowl in long, thin strips.

Add the potatoes and peas; 4 ounces ricotta salata, sliced; 1 cup sliced radishes; 3 tablespoons chopped fresh dill; 1 tablespoon extra-virgin olive oil; and 1 tablespoon fresh lemon juice. Season with salt and pepper, toss, and serve.

ALSO TRY:
cucumber + potatoes + feta + mint + peas

Grilled Asparagus + Sliced Potato Salad with Anchovy Butter

On a cutting board, chop together 3 tablespoons softened unsalted butter, 2 anchovy fillets, and 1 small finely grated garlic clove, until blended; season with salt and pepper.

Fill a large saucepan with water to a depth of 2 inches, add salt, and bring to a simmer over medium-low heat. Slice 4 medium Yukon Gold potatoes into ¼-inch-thick rounds and arrange them in a steamer basket; set the basket in the pan. Cover and steam the potatoes until tender, 10 to 12 minutes.

Meanwhile, preheat a grill pan over high heat. Drizzle 1 pound asparagus, trimmed, with 1 tablespoon olive oil; season with salt and pepper. Cook the asparagus in two batches on the hot grill pan until charred and tender, 2 to 3 minutes per batch. Cut the asparagus in half widthwise.

Arrange the warm potatoes and asparagus on a serving platter, season with pepper, and dollop with the butter mixture. Serve with lemon wedges.

ALSO TRY:
green beans + potatoes + chopped hard-boiled egg + garlic butter

Ground Lamb + Butternut Squash Salad with Chile-Cilantro Oil

Preheat the oven to 500°F with a rack in the bottom position.

Meanwhile, peel, seed, and thinly slice 1 small butternut squash (about 1½ pounds) into ¼-inch pieces; transfer to a baking sheet. Toss the squash with 1 tablespoon olive oil and ½ teaspoon chili powder, season with salt and pepper, and roast until it is tender and beginning to brown, about 15 minutes.

While the squash roasts, chop 2 fresh hot chiles and ¼ cup fresh cilantro (leaves from 1/2 bunch); set aside. Heat a large heavy skillet over medium-high heat. Add 8 ounces ground lamb and ½ teaspoon ground cumin, and cook, stirring, until the lamb is cooked through, about 5 minutes. Season with salt and pepper.

In a small bowl, stir together the cilantro, chiles, 3 tablespoons olive oil, and 1 tablespoon fresh lime juice. Rinse and dry 3 cups (2 ounces) baby arugula, place them on a serving platter, and scatter with the squash and lamb. Dollop with ¼ cup Greek yogurt and spoon the dressing over the top.

ALSO TRY:
crumbled turkey sausage + roasted sweet potato + parsley oil

Spicy Mussel Soup

Combine 2½ pounds mussels, scrubbed, debearded, and washed clean; 1 cup dry white wine; and ½ cup water in a Dutch oven or other large pot. Cover and bring to a boil over high heat; cook until the mussels have opened, 8 to 10 minutes (discard those that do not open).

Remove the mussels to a large bowl, leaving the liquid in the pot. Add to the liquid 3 chopped garlic cloves, 2 sliced fresh hot chiles, 1½ cups best-quality marinara sauce, and 2 tablespoons salted butter. Reduce the heat and simmer until the broth has thickened slightly and flavors are blended, about 3 minutes. Stir in ¼ cup chopped fresh parsley leaves and the reserved mussels. Season with salt and pepper to taste, and serve with crusty bread.

Greek Lemon + Egg Soup with Dandelion Greens

Bring 8 cups (2 quarts) vegetable broth to a boil in a Dutch oven or other large pot. Add 1¼ cups white long-grain rice and simmer until tender, about 15 minutes.

Meanwhile, in a medium bowl, toss 1 bunch dandelion greens, stems trimmed and leaves roughly torn, with the finely grated zest of 1 lemon, 2 tablespoons fresh lemon juice, 2 tablespoons olive oil, and salt and pepper until coated; set aside.

When the rice is tender, whisk together 4 large eggs and ¼ cup fresh lemon juice in a small bowl. While whisking the eggs, slowly add about ¼ cup hot broth from the pot. Remove the pot from the heat and transfer the warmed egg mixture from the bowl to the pot; stir until thickened and creamy, about 1 minute. Season with salt and pepper to taste and serve topped with the reserved greens.

OR TOP WITH:
sliced radicchio + shaved Pecorino Romano

Grilled Gazpacho

Preheat a grill to medium-high heat or a grill pan over medium-high heat.

Core and cut into large flat-sided pieces 6 medium plum tomatoes and 1 red bell pepper. Lightly oil the grill grates or pan, add the vegetables, and cook until charred, about 5 minutes.

Transfer the grilled vegetables to a food processor with 2 Kirby cucumbers, cut into chunks; ½ shallot; ½ cup fresh parsley leaves; 1 small garlic clove; and 1 teaspoon red wine vinegar. Season with salt and pepper and pulse to finely chop and blend. Serve with crusty bread.

ALSO TRY:
husked tomatillos + poblano + cucumbers + shallot + garlic + cilantro

Red Lentil Soup
with Browned Spice Butter

In a medium saucepan over high heat, combine 1 can (15 ounces) chopped tomatoes, with juice; 1½ cups dried red lentils, rinsed and drained; 2 crushed garlic cloves; ¼ cup peeled and sliced fresh ginger; 2 teaspoons curry powder; 1 cup water; and 4 cups chicken broth. Season with salt and pepper. Cover and bring the soup to a boil, then reduce to a simmer and cook, covered, until the lentils are almost tender, 8 to 10 minutes.

Meanwhile, melt 4 tablespoons salted butter in a small skillet over medium heat. Crush ½ teaspoon coriander seeds in a mortar with a pestle. Add them to the skillet with 1 teaspoon mustard seeds and cook, swirling the pan occasionally, until the butter is browned and the seeds are toasted, 1 to 2 minutes.

Add 2 tablespoons of the flavored butter to the soup and simmer 5 minutes more. Stir in 1 tablespoon fresh lemon juice, and remove the ginger pieces. Serve topped with a dollop of Greek yogurt (¼ cup total) and the remaining flavored butter.

Kale Farinata Soup with Fried Capers

Heat 2 tablespoons olive oil in a large saucepan over medium heat. Add 2 tablespoons capers, drained and patted dry, and cook until crispy, 2 minutes; remove with a slotted spoon and set aside. Add 1 chopped small onion, 2 chopped carrots, 2 chopped garlic cloves, and ½ teaspoon fennel seeds to the pan and cook, stirring, until the onion is tender, about 6 minutes.

Add 4 cups (1 quart) chicken broth, 2 cups water, and 1 can (15 ounces) chickpeas, drained and rinsed; cover and bring to a boil. Whisk in 4 cups chopped kale, then ¾ cup fine cornmeal; simmer until the kale is tender and the soup has thickened, about 3 minutes. Season the soup with salt and pepper, and serve topped with the capers and a drizzle of olive oil.

Pappa al Pomodoro (Tomato + Bread Soup)

Core and crush 6 medium tomatoes in a medium bowl. Warm 3 tablespoons olive oil in a large skillet over medium heat; add 2 sliced garlic cloves and cook until fragrant, 1 minute. Add the crushed tomatoes, 1 cup stale bread chunks, 1 cup water, and 2 sprigs fresh basil. Season with salt and pepper. Simmer until the tomatoes are saucy and the bread has softened and thickened the soup, 5 to 7 minutes. Remove the basil.

Serve the soup topped with freshly grated Parmesan cheese (about ½ cup total), a drizzle of olive oil, and a few more sprigs of fresh basil.

Simple Miso Soup with Asparagus, Edamame + Pan-Fried Tofu

Combine 6 cups water, 3 large pieces kombu (dried kelp) *— Found in Asian sections of specialty food markets*, and ½ teaspoon red pepper flakes in a medium saucepan and bring to a boil over high heat. Strain the broth and return it to the saucepan (discard the solids).

Cut ½ pound asparagus into 1-inch pieces, and stir it into the broth with the sliced whites of 4 scallions (slice and reserve the greens) and 1 cup shelled edamame *— fresh or frozen*. In a small heat-proof bowl, stir together ½ cup of the hot broth and ½ cup white miso; whisk this back into the broth in the pan. Simmer until the asparagus is just tender, about 2 minutes. Stir 1 teaspoon rice vinegar and 1 teaspoon soy sauce into the broth.

Meanwhile, heat 2 tablespoons vegetable oil in a medium skillet over medium heat. Press 1 package (14 ounces) firm tofu between layers of paper towel and top with a heavy skillet to drain out the liquid, then halve it crosswise and slice it into eight pieces. Add the tofu to the skillet and cook, turning occasionally, until it is seared on all sides, about 5 minutes. Divide the tofu among serving bowls and ladle the soup over the top. Sprinkle with the scallion greens.

Puréed Vegetable Soups
3 Ways

BASIC TECHNIQUE Bring the vegetables and 6 cups water to a boil in a medium saucepan over high heat; season with salt and pepper. Cook until the vegetables are tender, 5 to 10 minutes (depending on the type of vegetables). Stir in 2 tablespoons salted butter. Use a blender to purée soup in batches (keep the top cracked to prevent spattering), adding more water if necessary until the soup has the consistency of heavy cream. Stir in 1 tablespoon fresh lemon juice and adjust the salt and pepper to taste before serving. Serve with salad and crusty bread, if desired.

Asparagus Soup with Dill Oil

1 large potato, peeled and coarsely grated
1 medium onion, peeled and coarsely grated
2 strips lemon zest
2 bunches asparagus, trimmed and cut into 2-inch pieces

Just before serving, place ⅓ cup olive oil and ½ cup fresh dill fronds in a blender and blend until smooth. Spoon the dill oil over the soup.

Carrot-Ginger Soup

1 medium onion, peeled and coarsely grated
2 pounds carrots, peeled and coarsely grated
½ cup peeled and chopped fresh ginger

Just before serving, spoon a dollop of Greek yogurt into each bowl of soup.

Cauliflower Soup with Capers + Parsley

1 medium head cauliflower (2 pounds), coarsely chopped into florets
1 medium onion, peeled and coarsely grated
1 small floury potato, such as Russet, peeled and coarsely grated
1 tablespoon Dijon mustard

Just before serving, combine 1 tablespoon capers, ¼ cup chopped fresh parsley, and 2 tablespoons olive oil in a small bowl and spoon over the soup.

Serve with a simple salad.

Fava, Mint + Ricotta Crostino

Shell and peel 2 pounds fresh fava beans (to equal
2 cups beans). Bring ½ cup salted water to a boil in *or fresh or frozen peas*
a medium skillet. Add the beans, cover, and simmer
until tender, 2 to 5 minutes. Drain the beans and return
them to the skillet.

Toss the beans with 1 tablespoon olive oil, ½ teaspoon
red wine vinegar, and ¼ cup fresh mint leaves; season
with salt and pepper. Divide 1 cup ricotta cheese among
4 thick slices toasted crusty bread, spreading it evenly. *or dill*
Top with the bean mixture and serve.

Goat Cheese, Thyme + Charred Tomatoes on Toast

Preheat the broiler with a rack in the top position.

Place 4 whole plum tomatoes on a foil-lined baking sheet and broil until charred and beginning to burst, about 5 minutes. Set aside; discard the foil.

Split ½ medium baguette lengthwise and halve each piece widthwise to make four pieces total. Halve 1 garlic clove and rub the face of each piece with the cut side. Carefully smash one broiled tomato onto each piece of bread, using a fork to mash it in. Divide among the bread slices 4 ounces goat cheese, sliced, and top each with a sprig of fresh thyme. Drizzle each piece with olive oil and season with salt and pepper. Place on the baking sheet and broil until the goat cheese starts to brown, 2 to 3 minutes. Serve immediately.

Marinated Cucumber + Feta Sandwiches

With a vegetable peeler, shave 4 Kirby or Persian cucumbers into a medium bowl in long, thin strips. Toss the cucumbers with 1 small red onion, thinly sliced; 1 to 2 tablespoons sugar; ¼ cup red wine vinegar; and a generous pinch of salt. Let stand so the flavors combine, at least 10 minutes.

Meanwhile, split 4 sandwich rolls (such as ciabatta). Cut about 8 ounces feta cheese into four thick slices and place each on a roll. Squeeze the excess liquid from the marinated cucumber, divide it among the rolls, and serve.

ALSO TRY:
raw zucchini ribbons + halved cherry tomatoes + ricotta salata cheese

Radish, Watercress + Butter Sandwiches

Partially split 2 medium baguettes lengthwise (so one long side remains attached on each). Spread each half with 1 tablespoon softened salted butter (4 tablespoons total). Thinly slice 6 medium radishes and arrange the slices on each buttered baguette; divide 1 cup watercress among the sandwiches. Sprinkle with sea salt, slice into four pieces total, and serve.

ALSO TRY:
brie + pear + endive

Grilled Vegetable Sandwiches with Fresh Aioli

Preheat a grill to medium-high heat or a grill pan over medium-high heat.

Toss together 3 bell peppers, cored and cut into planks; 1 pound mixed summer squash (sliced ⅜ inch thick); and 1 small eggplant (sliced ⅜ inch thick) in a large bowl with 2 tablespoons olive oil and salt and pepper. Grill the vegetables, turning once, until tender, about 5 minutes for squash and eggplant, 8 minutes for peppers.

Meanwhile, combine 3 large egg yolks, ½ small garlic clove, and 2 tablespoons fresh lemon juice in a blender. With the motor running, slowly pour in ⅓ cup olive oil. Season the aioli with salt and pepper.

Split 4 sandwich rolls, fill each with vegetables, and top with the aioli. Serve immediately.

OR TOP WITH:
store-bought olive tapenade + fried eggs

Merguez Burgers with Cucumber Dressing

Preheat a grill to medium-high heat or a grill pan over medium-high heat.

Meanwhile, place 2 teaspoons fennel seeds, ½ teaspoon coriander seeds, and ½ teaspoon cumin seeds in a mortar and crush with a pestle. ← *Or put in a ziplock bag and bash with a rolling pin*

In a medium bowl, combine the spices with 1 pound ground lamb, 2 minced garlic cloves, 1 tablespoon harissa paste (or 1 teaspoon chili powder and ½ teaspoon paprika), 1½ teaspoons kosher salt, and ⅛ teaspoon ground cayenne pepper. Oil the grill grate or pan. Form the spiced meat into four 1½-inch thick patties and grill, turning once, until charred and cooked through, 4 to 5 minutes per side for medium doneness.

While the burgers are cooking, combine 3 sliced Kirby cucumbers, ¼ cup Greek yogurt, and 1 teaspoon red wine vinegar in a small bowl. Season with salt and pepper. Serve the burgers on rolls topped with the cucumber dressing.

OR TOP WITH:
tahini + lemon juice + roasted red peppers + mint

California-Style Salmon Burgers

Preheat the broiler with a rack in the top position. Line a baking sheet with foil.

In a food processor, combine 2 ounces stale bread (about 1 slice sandwich bread), torn into pieces, with 1 large egg white and pulse to form fine crumbs. Add 1 pound skinless salmon fillet, cut into pieces. Season with salt and pepper and pulse to finely chop the salmon. Form the mixture into four 3-inch patties (about 1½ inches thick).

Arrange the burgers on the baking sheet and broil until lightly browned on top and opaque throughout, about 5 minutes. Sandwich the burgers in buns with fresh sprouts, sliced red onion, and sliced avocado. Serve with lime wedges.

OR TOP WITH:
bacon + radicchio + lemon

Catfish Sandwiches with Radish Rémoulade

Heat ¼ cup vegetable oil in a large skillet over medium heat. Lightly beat 2 egg whites in a small bowl and season with salt and pepper. Place ½ cup cornmeal on a plate.

Dip 4 catfish fillets (about 6 ounces each) in the egg whites and then dredge in the cornmeal to coat. *or tilapia* Cook the fillets in the hot skillet, turning once, until opaque throughout and golden brown, about 3 minutes per side. Remove to a paper-towel-lined plate.

For the rémoulade, coarsely grate about 5 radishes and ½ small shallot, and stir together in a medium bowl with ½ cup mayonnaise, 1 tablespoon chopped fresh tarragon, and ½ teaspoon white wine vinegar; season with salt and pepper. Serve the catfish on rolls with the rémoulade and lettuce leaves.

Croques Madames Florentine

Preheat the broiler with a rack in the top position.

Melt 4 tablespoons salted butter in a medium saucepan over medium heat. Whisk in ¼ cup flour and, continuing to whisk, gradually add 3 cups milk. Bring to a boil, whisking occasionally. Reduce the heat and simmer 1 minute, then with a wooden spoon, stir in freshly grated nutmeg to taste and ½ cup grated Gruyère cheese. Set half of the sauce aside. To the remaining sauce in the pan, add 4 cups (8 ounces) fresh spinach, stir until wilted, then set aside.

About ⅛ teaspoon

Spread 8 slices sandwich bread with Dijon mustard (2 tablespoons total) and top 4 with 1 slice prosciutto (4 slices total) and the creamed spinach. Top with the remaining bread slices.

Melt 1 tablespoon salted butter in a large ovenproof skillet over medium heat. Cook the sandwiches in batches until browned on both sides, about 4 minutes per side. Top the sandwiches with the remaining white sauce and another ½ cup grated Gruyère cheese and transfer to the broiler; cook until the cheese is browned and bubbly, about 2 minutes.

Melt 1 tablespoon salted butter in a large nonstick skillet over medium heat. Crack 4 large eggs into the pan, and fry until the whites are set but the yolks are still runny, 3 to 4 minutes; season with salt and pepper. Top the sandwiches with the fried eggs and serve.

Serve with a simple salad.

Grilled Cheese 3 Ways

BASIC TECHNIQUE Make four sandwiches with 8 slices bread, cheese, and filling, placing any non-spreadable filling between the cheese slices.

Melt 2 tablespoons salted butter in a large nonstick skillet over medium heat, add two sandwiches, and place a smaller heavy skillet on top to weigh them down. Cook, flipping the sandwiches (and replacing the small skillet "weight") midway, until they are golden brown on both sides, about 8 minutes. Repeat with more butter and the remaining sandwiches.

Grilled Cheddar + Arugula Sandwiches

1 cup arugula leaves
8 thick slices sharp Cheddar cheese (about 8 ounces total)
¼ cup mayonnaise

Grilled Havarti Sandwiches with Pepperoncini

8 thick slices Havarti cheese (about 8 ounces total)
1 cup sliced pepperoncini or sweet-and-spicy pickled banana peppers
¼ cup grainy mustard

Grilled Fontina, Prosciutto + Apricot Sandwiches

8 ounces fontina cheese, thickly sliced
4 ounces thinly sliced prosciutto
¼ cup apricot preserves

Spaghetti with Ramps + Breadcrumbs

Bring a large pot of salted water to a boil and cook 1 pound spaghetti according to package directions. Drain the pasta (reserve ¼ cup pasta water) and set it aside.

Or use ⅔ cup panko

Meanwhile, in a food processor, pulse 2 slices stale bread (3 ounces) until coarse crumbs form. Chop the bulbs of 8 ounces ramps (reserve the greens).

Or a small bunch of scallions + 1 small garlic clove

In a large skillet, heat 1 tablespoon olive oil over medium heat; add the breadcrumbs and cook, stirring occasionally, until golden, about 5 minutes. Transfer the breadcrumbs to a bowl and season with salt and pepper; wipe the skillet with a paper towel.

Place 1 tablespoon olive oil and 2 tablespoons salted butter in the skillet and set it over medium heat. When the butter melts, add the ramps and cook until fragrant and tender, about 4 minutes. Add the pasta to the skillet with the cooked ramps, add the reserved greens, and toss until wilted. Stir in the reserved pasta water to create a thin sauce. Serve sprinkled with the breadcrumbs.

Spaghetti with Spicy Zucchini Marinara + Fresh Mozzarella

Bring a large pot of salted water to a boil and cook 1 pound spaghetti according to package directions. Drain the pasta and set it aside.

Meanwhile, halve lengthwise and thinly slice 6 small zucchini (about 1½ pounds total). Heat 2 tablespoons olive oil in a large skillet over medium heat, add 1 sliced garlic clove, and cook until fragrant, 1 minute. Add the zucchini and ½ teaspoon red pepper flakes, season with salt and pepper, and cook, stirring occasionally, until the zucchini are nearly tender, about 8 minutes. Add 1 cup best-quality marinara sauce and cook until heated through, 3 minutes.

In a serving bowl, toss the hot pasta with the sauce, ½ cup torn fresh basil leaves, and 8 ounces bocconcini.

Cherry-size mozzarella balls (or use chopped mozz)

Pasta Primavera

Bring a large pot of salted water to a boil and cook
1 pound egg tagliatelle according to package directions.
Drain the pasta (reserve ¼ cup pasta water) and return
it to the pot.

Meanwhile, heat 1 tablespoon salted butter and
1 tablespoon olive oil in a large skillet over medium-
high heat. Add 1 chopped garlic clove and cook until
fragrant, 30 seconds. Add 2 cups fresh peas; 1 pound
asparagus, trimmed and cut into ½-inch pieces; 2½ cups
quartered cremini mushrooms (8 ounces); and season
with salt and pepper. Cook, stirring, until the asparagus
is tender, 4 to 5 minutes. Add 4 cups (8 ounces) baby
beet greens to the skillet and stir until wilted.

or frozen peas, thawed

Try oyster mushrooms and/or shiitakes, too.

or baby spinach

Just before serving, toss the pasta with the
vegetables and 1 cup crème fraîche or sour cream.
Stir in the reserved pasta water if necessary for the
desired consistency. Grate Parmesan cheese over
the pasta, if desired, and serve.

Spaghetti with Braised Green Cabbage, Prosciutto + Olives

Bring a large pot of salted water to a boil and cook 1 pound spaghetti according to package directions. Drain the pasta (reserve ¼ cup pasta water) and return it to the pot.

Meanwhile, thinly slice ½ small head green cabbage. Heat 2 tablespoons salted butter in a large skillet over medium heat, and add the cabbage and ½ cup dry white wine. Cover and cook, stirring occasionally, until the wine is reduced by about half and the cabbage is tender and lightly browned, 12 to 15 minutes; during the last 5 minutes of cooking, add ½ cup olives, pitted and halved (about 10 whole olives), to the skillet.

Toss the cooked pasta with the cabbage and olives, and add 3 ounces thinly sliced prosciutto, pulled apart into long strips. If necessary, stir in the reserved pasta water to coat the pasta lightly. Season with salt and pepper and serve.

smash the olives with the bottom of a can to split and pit them.

ALSO TRY:
braised endive + capers + salami

Linguine with Braised Swiss Chard + Poached Egg

Bring a large pot of salted water to a boil and cook 1 pound linguine according to package directions. Drain the pasta, reserving enough water to refill the pot to a depth of 3 inches; keep the water at a simmer.

Meanwhile, slice 1 bunch Swiss chard, cutting stems into ½-inch pieces and leaves into 1-inch pieces. Heat 2 tablespoons olive oil in a large skillet over medium heat. Add the Swiss chard and 1 sliced garlic clove; season with salt and pepper. Cook, tossing, until the greens are wilted. Add 1 pint cherry tomatoes and ¼ cup balsamic vinegar, and cook, partially covered, until the greens are tender and the tomatoes have split slightly, about 10 minutes. Remove from the heat, add the pasta and 2 tablespoons olive oil, and toss until combined; cover and set aside.

Add 1 teaspoon white vinegar to the remaining pasta water. Crack 4 large eggs into the simmering *or crack each into a cup first* water, and poach until the whites are set but the yolks jiggle, 1 to 2 minutes; remove with a slotted spoon. Divide the pasta among four plates and top each with a poached egg. Season with salt and pepper and serve.

ALSO TRY:
collard greens + ¼ cup white wine + poached eggs

Fettuccine Puttanesca

Bring a large pot of salted water to a boil and cook 1 pound fettuccine according to package directions.

Meanwhile, heat 2 tablespoons olive oil in a medium skillet over medium-high heat. Add 2 sliced garlic cloves and cook until fragrant, about 30 seconds. Add 2 chopped anchovy fillets; 2 tablespoons capers, drained; ½ teaspoon red pepper flakes; and ½ cup Kalamata olives, pitted and halved (about 10 whole olives). Cook, stirring to break up the anchovies, for 2 minutes. Stir in 2 cups best-quality marinara sauce and simmer for 5 minutes. Stir in ¼ cup chopped fresh parsley leaves, toss the cooked pasta with the sauce until coated, and serve.

Smash the olives with the bottom of a can to split and pit them.

Linguine with Fresh Garlic Sauce

Bring a large pot of salted water to a boil and cook
1 pound linguine according to package directions. Drain
the pasta (reserve ¼ cup pasta water) and return it to
the pot.

or 2 cloves regular garlic

Meanwhile, chop the whites and greens of 1 head
fresh spring garlic (about 1 cup), and combine it with
1 teaspoon freshly grated lemon zest and ¼ cup olive oil
in a blender. Season generously with salt and pepper,
and blend to emulsify. Toss the sauce with the hot pasta
and, if needed, the reserved pasta water until coated.
Serve with lemon wedges.

ALSO TRY:
garlic cloves + small handful grated Parmesan + toasted, crushed
fennel seeds

Orzo Risotto with Pancetta + Radicchio

Place a medium saucepan over medium heat. Add 4 ounces chopped pancetta and cook until fat begins to render, about 2 minutes. Add 1 cup orzo and the leaves from 1 sprig fresh rosemary and cook, stirring, until the pancetta and orzo are golden, about 6 minutes. Meanwhile, heat 3 cups chicken broth in a small saucepan over low heat.

Add 1 cup hot broth to the orzo and quickly simmer over medium-high heat until the orzo is silky and the liquid has nearly evaporated, about 5 minutes. Repeat with the remaining 2 cups broth, adding a cup at a time and cooking until each addition has nearly evaporated. Stir in 2 cups sliced radicchio, and serve sprinkled with additional fresh rosemary leaves.

ALSO TRY:
orzo + bacon + fresh thyme + shredded Brussels sprouts

Pasta Handkerchiefs with Broccoli Rabe + Ricotta

Bring a large pot of salted water to a boil and cook 8 ounces fresh lasagna sheets, halved widthwise, according to package directions. Remove the cooked pasta with tongs to a colander to drain, leaving the water in the pot. Return the pasta water to a boil. Drizzle the pasta with olive oil to prevent sticking.

Heat 3 tablespoons olive oil in a large skillet over medium heat. Add 4 sliced garlic cloves and 1 teaspoon red pepper flakes and cook until the garlic is lightly toasted, 2 minutes.

Meanwhile, add 2 bunches broccoli rabe, halved widthwise, to the boiling pasta water and cook until crisp-tender, about 2 minutes. Remove the broccoli rabe from the water with the tongs and transfer it directly to the skillet. Cook, stirring, until the broccoli rabe is tender and any pasta water clinging to it has evaporated, about 3 minutes.

Divide the pasta among four plates, layering it with 1 cup ricotta and the broccoli rabe. Season with salt and pepper and drizzle with olive oil before serving.

Spaghetti Cacio e Pepe

Bring a large pot of salted water to a boil and cook
1 pound spaghetti according to package directions.
Drain the pasta (reserve ¾ cup pasta water) and   *Or regular black peppercorns*
return it to the pot.

Meanwhile, heat a small skillet over medium heat.
Place 2 teaspoons black peppercorns and 2 teaspoons
Szechuan peppercorns in the pan and toast until   *Or put in a ziplock bag and bash with a rolling pin*
fragrant, 2 to 3 minutes. Place the peppercorns in a
mortar and crush with a pestle until coarsely ground.
Transfer the pepper to a medium bowl with 3 large egg
yolks and 2 packed cups finely grated Pecorino Romano
cheese.

When the pasta is done, stir ½ cup of the reserved
pasta water into the egg mixture, add the pasta, and
toss to coat. Stir in the remaining pasta water, if needed,
to reach the desired consistency. Season with salt, and
serve immediately.

OR TOP WITH:
fresh or frozen (thawed) peas

Grilled Turkey Sausage + Pepper Pizza

To bake instead, follow the directions on page 90; cut the raw peppers into rings.

Preheat a grill to medium-high heat.

In a medium bowl, toss 1 pound mixed bell peppers, cored, seeded, and cut into planks (or baby bell peppers, cut in half), with 1 tablespoon olive oil, and season with salt and pepper. Grill, turning once, until crisp-tender and charred, about 4 minutes; set aside. *or a wine bottle*

Meanwhile, on a lightly floured surface with a lightly floured rolling pin, roll out 1 pound pizza dough into a large, thin rectangle about ¼ inch thick. Transfer to a cutting board sprinkled with flour or cornmeal. Scatter over the dough 1 ball (4 ounces) fresh mozzarella, torn into pieces, and 2 sweet Italian (raw) turkey sausages (about ½ pound total), removed from their casing and pinched into small pieces.

Oil the grill grates, place the reserved peppers on the pizza and slide it onto the grill. Cook, covered, until the sausage is opaque and the cheese is bubbling, 15 minutes. Sprinkle with red pepper flakes and fresh basil leaves to serve, if desired.

ALSO TRY:
ground lamb + grilled chiles + smoked mozzarella

Mussels Pizza Bianco

Preheat the oven to 475°F with a rack in the bottom position. Place a large rimmed baking sheet upside down on the rack to preheat, about 8 minutes.

Meanwhile, purée together 4 garlic cloves, 3 tablespoons grated Parmesan cheese, and *or a wine bottle* 2 tablespoons white wine in a blender.

On a lightly floured piece of parchment paper with a lightly floured rolling pin, roll 8 ounces pizza dough into a large rectangle, about ¼ inch thick. Spread the blended bianco sauce over the dough, leaving a 1-inch border. Top with 8 ounces mussels, scrubbed, debearded, and washed clean. Drizzle with olive oil, and sprinkle with 1 chopped fresh hot chile (optional).

Carefully remove the hot baking sheet from the oven and slide the parchment with the dough onto it. Bake until the dough is golden and crisp and the mussels are opened, 8 to 10 minutes. (Discard any mussels that do not open.) Before serving, sprinkle with ¼ cup fresh parsley leaves, and drizzle with more olive oil.

ALSO TRY:
clams + vodka + smashed cherry tomatoes + fresh chiles

Piadini with Pulled Bresaola, Baby Kale + Parmesan

Preheat the oven to 475°F with a rack in the bottom position. Place a large rimmed baking sheet upside down on the rack to preheat, about 8 minutes.

On a lightly floured piece of parchment paper, divide 8 ounces pizza dough into 4 portions; pat each into a thin round, about ¼ inch thick. Drizzle with olive oil and rub with the cut side of 1 halved garlic clove; season with salt and pepper.

Carefully remove the hot baking sheet from the oven and slide the parchment with the dough onto it. Bake until the dough is golden and crisp, 5 to 8 minutes.

Meanwhile, in a medium bowl, toss together 2 cups baby kale; 2 ounces bresaola, pulled apart; 1 ounce Parmesan cheese, shaved into thin pieces with a vegetable peeler (about ⅓ cup); 1 tablespoon olive oil; and 1 tablespoon balsamic vinegar. Season with salt and pepper.

Remove the piadini from the oven and, while they're still hot, divide the salad among them; fold each in half before serving.

Sliced cured beef, available in the deli aisle; you can use prosciutto instead

ALSO TRY:
baby greens + halved cherry tomatoes + olives + feta

Cast-Iron Pan Pizza with Pesto, Mozzarella + Salami

Preheat the broiler with a rack in the top position. Place a large (10-inch) cast-iron skillet over medium-high heat until hot, about 3 minutes. *Or a heavy-bottomed ovenproof skillet*

or a wine bottle On a lightly floured piece of parchment paper with a lightly floured rolling pin, roll 8 ounces pizza dough into a circle roughly 12 inches wide.

Place 2 tablespoons olive oil in the hot skillet. Transfer the dough to the skillet, carefully pressing the dough up the sides of the pan with a wooden spoon. Spread 3 tablespoons prepared pesto sauce over the pizza dough, then scatter with ½ cup coarsely grated low-moisture mozzarella (about 2 ounces) and 2 ounces thinly sliced salami, torn into pieces. Broil until the dough is cooked, the cheese is bubbly, and the salami is browned in spots, 4 to 5 minutes.

ALSO TRY:
marinara sauce + olives + provolone + cooked, crumbled Italian sausage

Serve with a simple salad and store-bought hummus.

Grilled Flatbread with Feta, Lemon, Sesame Seeds + Fresh Oregano

or a wine bottle ↘

Preheat a 10- to 12-inch grill pan over medium-high heat.

On a lightly floured piece of parchment paper with a lightly floured rolling pin, roll 4 ounces pizza dough into a rectangle or circle to fit the grill pan. Rub the top of the dough with 1 tablespoon olive oil; season with salt and pepper.

When the pan is hot, oil it and place the dough in the pan oiled-side up. Cook until charred on the bottom, about 3 minutes. Flip the flatbread and top it with 1 ounce crumbled feta cheese, ½ teaspoon finely grated lemon zest, ½ teaspoon sesame seeds, and 1 tablespoon fresh oregano leaves. Grill the flatbread until cooked through, 1 to 2 minutes more.

Transfer the flatbread to a cutting board, cut it into four pieces, and serve.

ALSO TRY:
chopped garlic + fresh rosemary + ricotta

Alsatian Bacon + Egg Tart

Preheat the oven to 475°F with a rack in the bottom position. Place a large rimmed baking sheet upside down on the rack to preheat, about 8 minutes.

or a wine bottle ↘

On a lightly floured piece of parchment paper with a lightly floured rolling pin, roll 8 ounces pizza dough into a large rectangle, about ¼ inch thick. Scatter over the dough ½ small onion, very thinly sliced, and 4 thick slices bacon, cut into ½-inch pieces.

Carefully remove the hot baking sheet from the oven and slide the parchment with the dough onto it. Bake until the bacon is crisp, about 10 minutes.

Meanwhile, whisk together 2 large eggs and ½ cup sour cream in a medium bowl. Drizzle over the tart and bake until the egg mixture has set, about 5 minutes. Season with salt and pepper and serve.

Pizza 6 Ways

BASIC TECHNIQUE Preheat the oven to 475°F with a rack in the bottom position. Place a large rimmed baking sheet upside down on the rack to preheat, 8 minutes.

    On a piece of parchment paper dusted with *← or a wine bottle* cornmeal, using a lightly floured rolling pin, roll 1 pound pizza dough into a large circle, about ¼ inch thick. Scatter it with toppings. Carefully remove the hot baking sheet from the oven and slide the parchment with the dough onto it. Bake until the dough is golden and crisp, 8 to 10 minutes. Before serving, add the remaining fresh ingredients (or as directed), a drizzle of olive oil, and a sprinkle of sea salt.

Speck + Arugula Pizza

2 medium tomatoes, cored and crushed
6 ounces fresh mozzarella cheese, pulled apart

Just before serving, scatter with 2 cups baby arugula and 3 ounces thinly sliced speck.

← Like prosciutto but smoked

Summer Tomato + Fresh Chile Pizza

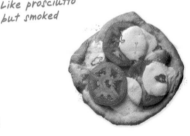

8 ounces mozzarella cheese, in thick slices
1 ripe, beautiful beefsteak tomato, in thick slices

Just before serving, scatter with 1 sliced fresh chile.

Ricotta, Pepper + Basil Pizza

1 cup fresh ricotta cheese
½ cup roasted red peppers, pulled apart
1 garlic clove, sliced

Just before serving, scatter with fresh basil leaves.

Three-Onion Pizza

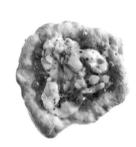

1 small yellow onion, thinly sliced
1 small red onion, thinly sliced
1 shallot, thinly sliced
1 tablespoon fresh thyme leaves
1 tablespoon olive oil

Crushed Tomato, Anchovy + Provolone Pizza

1 cup cherry or grape tomatoes, crushed
3 thick slices provolone cheese (2 ounces)
4 whole anchovy fillets
¼ teaspoon red pepper flakes

Leek + Parsley Pizza with Lemon + Olive Oil

2 medium leeks, white and light green parts thinly sliced
½ cup grated Pecorino Romano cheese
1 tablespoon olive oil

Just before serving, scatter with ¼ cup fresh parsley leaves and a squeeze of fresh lemon juice.

Serve with a simple salad.

Omelets with Asparagus + Fresh Goat Cheese

Bring ¼ cup salted water to a boil in a medium nonstick skillet over medium heat. Add 1 bunch asparagus, trimmed, and cover and steam until bright green and crisp-tender, 3 to 5 minutes. Transfer to a plate, wipe the skillet with a paper towel, and set the skillet aside.

In a large bowl, whisk together 8 large eggs and ¼ cup water; season with salt and pepper. Melt 1 tablespoon salted butter in the reserved skillet over medium heat. Add a quarter of the egg mixture and about 1 tablespoon chopped dill fronds and cook, pulling the edges of the eggs toward the center of the pan with a heat-proof spatula, until fully set, about 3 minutes. Add a quarter of the cooked asparagus and ¼ cup crumbled fresh goat cheese. Slide the omelet onto a plate, folding it over the asparagus and cheese.

Make three more omelets using the remaining egg mixture, asparagus, and an additional 3 tablespoons butter, 3 tablespoons chopped fresh dill fronds, and ¾ cup cheese. Serve immediately.

OR TOP WITH:
green beans + feta + fresh basil

Shakshuka

Heat 2 tablespoons olive oil in a large skillet over medium-high heat. Add 2 sliced garlic cloves and cook until fragrant, 1 minute. Stir in 2 teaspoons paprika and 1 teaspoon ground cumin, and toast the spices for 1 minute. Stir in 2 cups best-quality marinara sauce and bring to a simmer.

Use the back of a wooden spoon to make eight small wells in the sauce. Crack an egg into each well (8 large eggs total), cover, and cook until the eggs are set, 5 to 6 minutes. Season with salt and pepper and serve with pita bread.

Celery Root Rösti
with Gruyère + Eggs

Preheat the broiler with a rack in the top position.

Coarsely grate into a medium bowl 1 small peeled celery root (about 10 ounces) and 1 medium peeled potato; toss with 1 tablespoon cornstarch and leaves from 2 sprigs fresh rosemary. Season generously with salt and pepper.

Heat ¼ cup olive oil in a large nonstick ovenproof skillet over medium-high heat. Add the celery root mixture, pat it into a large pancake, and cook until browned on the underside, 5 to 7 minutes. Slide the pancake onto a plate, then carefully flip it back into the skillet to brown the other side, 5 to 7 minutes. Remove the skillet from the heat.

Crack 4 large eggs on top of the pancake, sprinkle with 2 ounces grated Gruyère cheese, and season with salt and pepper. Broil until the cheese is golden and bubbly and the egg whites are set, 3 to 5 minutes.

ALSO TRY:
parsnip + fresh thyme + prosciutto + Parmesan

Tomatillo Huevos Rancheros

Preheat the broiler with a rack in the top position.

Place on a rimmed baking sheet 2 unpeeled garlic cloves, the whole whites of 4 scallions (reserve the greens), and 1 pound tomatillos, husks removed. Broil until charred, about 3 minutes. Remove and discard the garlic skins and transfer the garlic, scallions (whites and greens), and tomatillos to a blender. Season with salt and pepper and pulse to chop into a coarse salsa; set aside.

Heat 1 tablespoon vegetable oil in a medium ovenproof skillet over medium-high heat. Add the salsa and 1 can (15 ounces) black beans, rinsed and drained, and cook for 3 minutes. Press down firmly on the bean mixture with the back of a wooden spoon, to make four small wells. Crack an egg into each well (4 large eggs total) and top with 4 ounces coarsely grated Pepper Jack cheese. Broil until egg whites are set, 3 to 5 minutes, then sprinkle with ¼ cup fresh cilantro leaves, and serve.

ALSO TRY:
plum tomatoes + pinto beans + Cheddar

Baked Eggs with Greens + Cheddar

Preheat the broiler with a rack in the middle position. Arrange four 8- to 10-ounce ramekins or custard cups on a rimmed baking sheet.

Heat 1 tablespoon olive oil in a medium skillet over medium-high heat. Add 8 cups baby kale and cook, *or baby spinach* tossing occasionally, until wilted, about 2 minutes; season with salt and pepper. Cut ½ medium baguette into ½-inch-thick slices.

Divide the greens among the ramekins and top each with a baguette slice and a slice of Cheddar cheese (4 ounces total). Crack an egg into each ramekin (4 large eggs total), season with salt and pepper, and broil, rotating the pan twice, until the egg whites are set, about 8 minutes.

ALSO TRY:
mushrooms + baguette + crème fraîche + grated nutmeg

Spaghetti Frittata with Spinach, Prosciutto + Mozzarella

Preheat the oven to 425°F.

Heat 2 tablespoons olive oil in a large ovenproof skillet over medium-high heat. Add 6 cups loosely packed baby spinach and cook until wilted, about 2 minutes. Stir in 3 cups leftover cooked spaghetti; 6 slices prosciutto (3 ounces), torn; and 8 ounces cubed fresh mozzarella cheese.

Whisk together 4 large eggs and ¼ cup grated Parmesan cheese in a medium bowl; season with salt and pepper. Add the egg mixture to the spaghetti mixture in the skillet and stir to combine. Transfer to the oven and bake the frittata until it is set throughout and browned in spots, about 15 minutes. Slice into wedges and serve.

ALSO TRY:
kale + cooked rice + coarsely grated sharp Cheddar

Egg Sandwiches 3 Ways

BASIC TECHNIQUE Toast 8 slices bread or 4 split English muffins. Divide the sandwich fillings among four slices of the bread or the English muffin bottoms. Melt 1 tablespoon salted butter in a large nonstick skillet over medium heat, and crack in 4 large eggs; fry until whites are set but yolks are still runny, 3 to 4 minutes. Season the eggs with salt and pepper, transfer them to the sandwiches, top with the remaining bread, and serve.

Baby Spinach, Avocado + Sriracha Egg Sandwiches

1 cup baby spinach
½ medium avocado, peeled, pitted, and sliced
2 teaspoons Sriracha sauce

Cheddar, Roasted Red Pepper + Balsamic Egg Sandwiches

4 thick slices Cheddar cheese (4 ounces)
½ cup roasted red peppers
1 teaspoon balsamic vinegar, for drizzling

Smashed Pea, Watercress + Fresh Mozzarella Egg Sandwiches

1 cup frozen peas, thawed, mashed, and seasoned with salt and pepper
1 cup watercress sprigs
4 ounces fresh mozzarella cheese, sliced

Steak with Herb Sauce + Buttered Radishes

Preheat the oven to 475°F.

Cut about 20 radishes into quarters (to yield 3 cups). Set aside.

Heat 1 tablespoon olive oil in a large ovenproof skillet over medium-high heat. Blot dry 1½ pounds London broil steak with a paper towel and season on both sides with salt and pepper. When the skillet is hot, add the steak and brown on both sides, about 3 minutes per side. Transfer the skillet to the oven and roast until the steak reaches the desired doneness, 6 to 8 minutes for medium-rare. Let the meat rest on a cutting board.

While the steak roasts, combine in a small bowl ½ cup chopped fresh herbs (such as mint, parsley, and cilantro), 1 small minced garlic clove, ¼ cup olive oil, and 2 tablespoons red wine vinegar. Season with salt and pepper and set the herb sauce aside. Heat 2 tablespoons salted butter in a medium skillet over medium-high heat, add the radishes, and cook, tossing occasionally, until lightly browned and crisp-tender, 6 to 8 minutes. Season with salt.

Slice the steak, top with the herb sauce, and serve with the radishes.

Grilled Lamb Chops with Cucumber, Oregano + Feta

Preheat a grill to medium-high heat or a grill pan over medium-high heat. Lightly oil the grill grates.

Blot dry 4 lamb shoulder or rib chops (about 1 inch thick) with a paper towel and season with salt and pepper. Place on the hot grill and cook until desired doneness, 6 to 8 minutes per side for medium-rare.

Meanwhile, halve and thickly slice 6 Kirby cucumbers (about 1 pound), and combine them in a large bowl with 1 tablespoon fresh oregano leaves, 4 ounces crumbled feta cheese, 2 teaspoons olive oil, and 1 teaspoon red wine vinegar. Season the cucumber salad with salt and pepper, and serve with the lamb chops.

OR TOP WITH:
thinly sliced fennel + olives + lemon juice

Grilled Lamb Kebabs with Eggplant + Plum Tomatoes

Preheat a grill to medium-high heat or a large grill pan over medium-high heat.

Combine 2 tablespoons fresh lemon juice, 1 minced garlic clove, and 1 tablespoon olive oil in a large bowl; season with salt and pepper. Add 1 pound boneless leg of lamb, cut into 1-inch pieces, and 2 small eggplants, cut into 1-inch pieces, and toss to coat. Thread the lamb and eggplant pieces onto eight 6-inch metal skewers.

Grill the kebabs, turning occasionally, until the lamb is cooked to medium-rare and the eggplant is tender, about 10 minutes. Remove from the grill and let rest 5 minutes. Meanwhile, grill 4 plum tomatoes, halved lengthwise, and 4 pita breads, brushed with oil, until slightly charred, about 3 minutes; season with salt and pepper.

Serve the kebabs with the pita, tomatoes, and a dollop of store-bought pesto sauce (¼ cup total).

Soak wooden skewers in water for 30 minutes first.

ALSO TRY:
chicken thighs + zucchini + tomatoes + store-bought olive tapenade

Sage-Rubbed Pork Chops with Grilled Peaches + Onions

Preheat a grill to medium-high heat or a grill pan over medium-high heat.

Place 1 tablespoon coarsely chopped fresh sage leaves and 1 teaspoon kosher salt in a mortar and crush with a pestle (or chop-mash against a cutting board with a chef's knife). Rub the sage salt over 4 bone-in pork chops (about 1 inch thick, 2 pounds total); season with pepper.

Lightly oil the grill grates or pan, add the pork chops, and grill until charred and just cooked through, 7 to 8 minutes per side. Let rest on a platter for a few minutes.

Meanwhile, in a medium bowl, toss together 2 firm peaches, pitted and halved; 1 small red onion, thickly sliced; and 1 tablespoon olive oil until coated. Season with salt and pepper. Place the peaches and onions on the grill and cook, turning, until they are charred and tender, 3 to 5 minutes. Serve the pork chops with the peaches and onions alongside.

OR TOP WITH:
grilled plums + shallots

Roasted Pork Tenderloin with Seckel Pears + Pistachios

Preheat the oven to 425°F.

Combine ½ teaspoon ground cardamom, ¼ teaspoon ground coriander, 1 tablespoon sea salt, and ½ teaspoon freshly ground black pepper in a small bowl. Rub the spice mixture on a 1½-pound pork tenderloin, patted dry and trimmed. Heat 2 tablespoons olive oil in a large skillet over high heat until very hot. Add the pork and sear, turning occasionally, until browned on all sides, *Or small Bartletts* about 8 minutes.

Meanwhile, halve 7 Seckel pears and set aside. Stir together 1 tablespoon honey and 1 teaspoon water in a cup. When the pork is browned, add the pears to the skillet, and toss. Transfer the skillet to the oven and roast 5 minutes. Remove, toss in ¼ cup shelled pistachios with the pears, and drizzle half of the honey mixture over the pork and brush to coat. Return the skillet to the oven and roast until the pork is barely pink in the center, 5 minutes.

Brush the pork with the remaining honey mixture and slice. Toss 1 tablespoon salted butter with the pears and pistachios in the skillet, and serve.

ALSO TRY:
pork tenderloin + seedless red grapes + walnuts

Seared Pork Chops with Blood Orange, Mint + Wilted Radicchio

Peel, quarter, and slice 4 blood oranges; set them aside. Quarter and core 1 medium head radicchio (about 12 ounces) and set it aside, too.

Heat 1 tablespoon olive oil in a large skillet over medium-high heat. Season 4 thinly sliced pork chops (¾ pound total) with salt and pepper. Add the pork to the skillet and sear, turning once, until browned and cooked through, 3 to 4 minutes total; set aside.

Add the oranges, radicchio, and 1 tablespoon honey to the hot skillet, plus more oil if necessary, and toss together until the radicchio wilts. Stir in 1 teaspoon white wine vinegar and ¼ cup fresh mint leaves and serve over the chops.

ALSO TRY:
pork cutlets + grapefruit + honey + frisée + fresh rosemary leaves

Roasted Sausage with Warm Bean + Kale Salad

Preheat the oven to 400°F.

Heat 1 tablespoon olive oil in a large ovenproof skillet over high heat. Add 4 sweet Italian pork sausages (about 1 pound total) and cook, turning, until browned on all sides, about 5 minutes.

While the sausages cook, rinse and chop 1 bunch kale leaves.

Remove the browned sausages from the skillet and set them aside. Add 1 tablespoon olive oil, 2 sliced garlic cloves, and 1 anchovy fillet to the skillet and cook, stirring, 1 minute. Stir in the kale and 1 can (15 ounces) cannellini beans, drained and rinsed. Top the kale mixture with the sausages and transfer the skillet to the oven. Bake until the sausages are opaque throughout, about 12 minutes.

or ½ teaspoon anchovy paste

Before serving, slice the sausages, toss with 1 tablespoon fresh lemon juice and drizzle with additional olive oil, if desired.

ALSO TRY:
sweet Italian sausage + Swiss chard + hazelnuts

Roasted Sausage Meatballs with Fennel + Tomatoes

Preheat the oven to 450°F.

Heat 1 tablespoon olive oil in a large ovenproof skillet over high heat. Remove from their casings 4 sweet Italian pork sausages (about 1 pound total). Pinch the meat into 1-inch balls, place them in the hot skillet, and brown all over, about 5 minutes.

Meanwhile, core and thinly slice 1 small fennel bulb (reserve ¼ cup fennel fronds). When the meatballs have browned, add the sliced fennel, 1 cup cherry tomatoes, and 1 teaspoon fennel seeds and toss until coated; season with salt and pepper.

Transfer the skillet to the oven and cook until the meatballs are opaque throughout and the fennel is tender, 10 to 12 minutes. Before serving, toss with 2 tablespoons fresh lemon juice and the reserved fennel fronds. Serve with crusty bread.

ALSO TRY:
sausage meatballs + halved Brussels sprouts + cherry tomatoes + fresh thyme

Colcannon

Fill a large saucepan with salted water to a depth of
2 inches and bring to a simmer over medium-low heat.
Peel, halve, and thinly slice 3 baking potatoes, arrange
them in a steamer basket, and set the basket in the
saucepan. Cover and steam the potatoes until almost
tender, 10 to 12 minutes. Meanwhile, rinse and chop
1 bunch kale.

Add the kale to the almost-tender potatoes, cover,
and continue to steam until the potatoes are cooked
through, 5 minutes. Transfer the potatoes to a large
bowl, and set the kale aside.

Mash the potatoes with ½ cup milk and 2 tablespoons
salted butter. Stir in 8 ounces chopped cooked ham
and the reserved kale; season generously with salt and
pepper and serve immediately.

OR TOP WITH:
a fried egg

Grilled Chicken Cutlets with Grapefruit + Watercress Salad

Preheat a grill to medium-high heat or a grill pan over medium-high heat.

Peel and segment 2 grapefruit, and set aside. Squeeze 2 tablespoons grapefruit juice from the remaining membranes; set aside. *Or a heavy skillet*

Using a flat meat mallet, pound 8 chicken cutlets (about 2 pounds total) to ¼-inch thickness. Season with salt and pepper. Lightly oil the grill grates, then grill the chicken, turning once, until cooked through, 2 to 3 minutes.

In a serving bowl, whisk together 2 tablespoons olive oil, ½ teaspoon grated peeled fresh ginger, and the reserved grapefruit juice in a serving bowl. Toss with the reserved grapefruit segments and 2 bunches watercress, thick stems trimmed. Serve the grilled cutlets with the salad.

OR TOP WITH:
lemon + blackberries + baby arugula

Breaded Chicken Cutlets with Pea Salad

Or mash it with a spoon in a small bowl

Place ¼ cup Dijon mustard, 1 tablespoon fresh tarragon leaves, and 1 tablespoon olive oil in a mortar and grind with a pestle until the tarragon is evenly distributed throughout the mustard. Season the mixture with salt and pepper, and transfer to a shallow dish. Place 1 cup panko breadcrumbs in another shallow dish.

Heat ¼ cup olive oil in a large skillet over medium heat. Dip 4 chicken cutlets (about 1 pound total) in the mustard mixture, allowing the excess to drip off, then dredge each in the panko. Add the cutlets to the hot skillet and cook, turning once, until browned and cooked through, 6 to 8 minutes total. Remove to a paper-towel-lined plate to drain.

While the chicken cooks, cut 6 ounces snap peas into ½-inch pieces and place in a large bowl with 3 cups pea tendrils. Add 1 tablespoon olive oil, season with salt and pepper, and toss to coat. Serve the chicken cutlets and salad with lemon wedges.

Aka "pea shoots"

OR TOP WITH:
cucumber ribbons + frozen (thawed) peas

Grilled Chicken Thighs with Herbed Tomato Salad

Preheat a grill to medium-high heat or a grill pan over medium-high heat.

Season 8 bone-in, skin-on chicken thighs (about 2 pounds total) with salt and pepper. Lightly oil the grill grates, then grill the chicken, turning once, until cooked through, about 5 minutes per side.

Meanwhile, cut 1 pound tomatoes into bite-size pieces. Combine the tomatoes in a medium bowl with 2 tablespoons coarsely chopped mixed fresh herbs (such as thyme, parsley, dill, and oregano) and 1 tablespoon capers, drained. Drizzle the tomato salad with olive oil, season with salt and pepper, and toss. Serve the chicken with the tomato salad.

Try a mix of heirloom tomatoes.

Lentils with Turkey Sausage + Fried Sage

Heat 1 tablespoon olive oil in a large skillet over medium-high heat. Add 4 sweet Italian (raw) turkey sausages (about 1 pound total) and cook, turning, until browned on all sides, about 8 minutes; set aside. Add 12 fresh sage leaves to the hot fat in the skillet and cook until crisp, about 2 minutes. Leaving the fat in the skillet, transfer the sage leaves to a paper-towel-lined plate to drain.

Add to the skillet 2 tablespoons olive oil and 2 chopped garlic cloves and cook until fragrant, 1 minute. Stir in 2 cans (15 ounces each) lentils, drained and rinsed; cook until heated through, about 2 minutes. Stir in 1 tablespoon fresh lemon juice and season with salt and pepper. Slice the sausage and serve with the lentils, fried sage, and crusty bread.

ALSO TRY:
Navy beans + Italian sausage + fried rosemary

Shrimp + Grits

Heat 1 tablespoon olive oil in a large skillet over medium-high heat. Add 1 small sliced onion; 1 small red bell pepper, cored and sliced; and 2 sliced garlic cloves and cook, tossing frequently, until crisp-tender, about 5 minutes.

Add 1 cup halved cherry tomatoes and ½ cup chicken broth and cook for 2 minutes. Add ½ pound peeled and deveined medium shrimp and cook until the shrimp are pink, 3 to 4 minutes. Remove from the heat and season with salt and pepper. Stir in ¼ teaspoon hot sauce and 2 tablespoons chopped fresh parsley.

Meanwhile, bring 3 cups chicken broth to a boil in a medium saucepan. Reduce the heat to a simmer, add 1 cup instant grits, and cook, stirring occasionally, until the broth is absorbed and the grits are tender, 3 to 5 minutes.

Serve the shrimp over the grits with additional hot sauce, if desired.

Seared Salmon with Orange-Rosemary Lentils

from 1 medium orange

Combine 1 cup cooked or canned lentils, ½ cup fresh orange juice, and leaves from 1 small sprig fresh rosemary in a small saucepan. Place over low heat and simmer until warmed through, 2 to 3 minutes. Meanwhile, peel and segment 2 oranges. Stir the segments into the warmed lentils, and season with salt and pepper. Cover and set aside.

Heat 2 teaspoons olive oil in a large skillet over medium-high heat. Add 4 salmon fillets (6 ounces each) and cook, turning once, until golden and just cooked through, 3 to 4 minutes per side.

Serve the salmon with the lentils alongside.

Grilled Sardines + Polenta with Onions + Raisins

Preheat a grill to medium-high heat.

Arrange 2 sliced medium onions, 1 tablespoon white wine vinegar, 1 cup raisins, and 3 tablespoons salted butter on a large piece of foil; season with salt and pepper. Fold the foil into a packet and crimp the edges to seal. Place the packet on the grill and cook, shaking occasionally, until the onions are tender, 12 to 14 minutes.

Meanwhile, season 12 medium sardines (about 2 pounds total), cleaned with heads and tails intact, with salt and pepper. Cut 1 tube (18 ounces) prepared polenta into 1-inch slices. Lightly oil the grill grates. Grill the polenta slices until charred on both sides, 3 to 4 minutes total. Brush the sardines with oil and grill them until charred on both sides and flaky, 5 to 8 minutes total. Serve the sardines with the grilled polenta; top with the onion mixture.

Baked Fish in Packets 3 Ways

BASIC TECHNIQUE Preheat the oven to 350°F.

Arrange four large pieces of parchment or foil on a work surface and place each of 4 fish fillets (tilapia, trout, or catfish; 1 to 1½ pounds total) in the center of each; season with salt and pepper. Dividing evenly, scatter the fish with the toppings.

Fold the edges of the parchment (or crinkle and gather if using foil) to create packets. Transfer the packets to a rimmed baking sheet and bake until the fish is cooked through, 12 to 15 minutes.

Baked Fish with Browned Butter + Balsamic Vinegar

2 tablespoons balsamic vinegar
2 tablespoons cold salted butter, cut into pieces

Baked Fish with Cherry Tomatoes, Chile + Ginger

2 cups cherry tomatoes
1 sliced hot fresh chile
2 tablespoons peeled, chopped fresh ginger
1 tablespoon olive oil

Baked Fish with Oranges + Olives

1 navel orange, unpeeled and sliced into rounds
1 cup pitted green olives ←
¼ cup fresh parsley leaves
1 tablespoon olive oil

Smash the olives with the bottom of a can to split and pit them.

serve with crusty bread.

Mussels + Sausage 3 Ways

BASIC TECHNIQUE Chop 1 medium onion and 2 garlic cloves. Place 1 tablespoon olive oil in a Dutch oven or other large pot over high heat. Add the onion and garlic and cook, stirring occasionally, until softened, about 5 minutes. Remove the sausages from their casings, breaking the meat in pieces into the pot, and cook, stirring occasionally, until crumbled and brown, about 3 minutes. Add 2 pounds mussels (scrubbed, debearded, and washed clean) and the remaining ingredients. Cover and bring to a boil, then reduce to a simmer and cook until the mussels have opened, 8 to 10 minutes (discard those that do not open).

Mussels + Sausage in Mustard Beer Broth

2 hot Italian sausages (about ½ pound)
1 tablespoon Dijon mustard
1 cup wheat beer

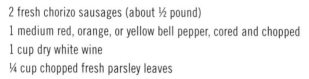

Mussels +
Fresh Chorizo
with Parsley + Peppers

2 fresh chorizo sausages (about ½ pound)
1 medium red, orange, or yellow bell pepper, cored and chopped
1 cup dry white wine
¼ cup chopped fresh parsley leaves

Mussels +
Sweet Sausage
with Lemon + Cream

2 sweet Italian sausages (about ½ pound)
4 strips lemon zest
1 cup heavy cream

Just before serving, stir in 2 tablespoons fresh lemon juice.

Roasted Haloumi, Scallions + Cherry Tomatoes with Couscous

Preheat the oven to 450°F.

On a large rimmed baking sheet, toss together 2 pints cherry tomatoes, 1 bunch scallions, left whole, and 2 sliced garlic cloves with 1 tablespoon olive oil; season with salt and pepper. Place 1 pound haloumi cheese, sliced ½ inch thick, among the tomatoes and scallions. Roast until the scallions are browned and some tomatoes have burst, about 10 minutes.

A salty, semi-hard cheese with a high melting point; available at specialty food markets

Meanwhile, prepare 1 box (10 ounces) plain couscous according to package directions. Set aside, covered.

Before serving, fluff the couscous with a fork. Serve the couscous topped with the haloumi and vegetables.

Curried Chickpeas with Rice

Prepare 1 cup uncooked white or brown rice according to package directions (or reheat 3 cups cooked rice).

Meanwhile, heat ¼ cup vegetable oil in a large skillet over medium-high heat. Add 1 tablespoon grated peeled fresh ginger, ½ teaspoon ground turmeric, 2 large finely chopped garlic cloves, ½ teaspoon garam masala, ¼ teaspoon ground cayenne pepper, ¼ teaspoon ground black pepper, and salt to taste and toast, stirring constantly, until fragrant, about 2 minutes. Stir in 1 can (28 ounces) diced tomatoes, with their juice; 2 cans (15 ounces each) chickpeas, drained and rinsed; and ¼ cup water and simmer until flavors blend, 10 minutes.

Divide the rice and chickpeas among four bowls and top each with a sprinkle of chopped fresh cilantro (2 tablespoons total).

White Bean + Escarole Ragù with Harissa Oil

Heat ¼ cup olive oil in a large skillet over medium heat. *[or 1 teaspoon chili powder and ½ teaspoon paprika]* Add 2 tablespoons harissa paste and cook, stirring, until fragrant, about 2 minutes. Pour off 2 tablespoons of the oil into a small heat-proof bowl, and set aside.

Add 4 sliced garlic cloves to the oil in the skillet and cook until golden, about 2 minutes. Add 1 can (14.5 ounces) diced tomatoes, with their juice; 2 cans *[or cannellinis]* (15 ounces each) navy beans, rinsed and drained; and 1 cup water. Cover and simmer the bean mixture for 5 minutes, then stir in 10 cups torn escarole (from 1 large head). Cover and simmer the ragù until thickened, about 10 minutes; season with salt and pepper.

Meanwhile, prepare 1 box (10 ounces) plain couscous according to package directions. Set aside, covered.

Before serving, fluff the couscous with a fork. Serve the ragù over the couscous, drizzled with the reserved harissa oil.

ALSO TRY:
chili powder + black-eyed peas + collard greens + white rice + hot sauce

Potato Latkes with Sautéed Apples + Thyme

Coarsely grate 2 medium unpeeled potatoes and 1 small onion into a medium bowl. Stir in 1 large beaten egg and season generously with salt and pepper.

Heat ¼ cup vegetable oil in a large skillet over medium-high heat. Working in two batches, spoon the potato mixture into the skillet and pat to flatten into small cakes (about ½ cup per latke). Cook, flipping once, until golden on both sides, about 8 minutes per batch. Transfer to a paper-towel-lined plate to drain.

While the latkes cook, core and cut into wedges 3 firm, sweet apples. Heat 1 tablespoon vegetable oil in a medium skillet over medium heat, add the apples and 3 sprigs fresh thyme, and season with salt and pepper. Cook, tossing, until tender, about 8 minutes. Serve the warm latkes with the apples.

I like Galas.

OR TOP WITH:
sautéed pears + golden raisins + fresh rosemary

Polenta with Mushrooms + Taleggio

Preheat the broiler with a rack in the top position.

Bring 2 cups water to a boil in a medium ovenproof saucepan with 2 tablespoons salted butter and ½ teaspoon salt. Whisk in 1 cup coarse cornmeal and simmer, stirring occasionally, until tender, about 15 minutes.

Meanwhile, heat 2 teaspoons olive oil in a large skillet over medium-high heat. Add 1 pound mixed mushrooms, halved (quartered, if large), and leaves from 2 sprigs fresh rosemary, season with salt and pepper, and cook, tossing occasionally, until the mushrooms are browned and tender, 8 to 10 minutes.

Spoon the mushrooms over the polenta in the saucepan and top with 4 ounces sliced Taleggio cheese. Transfer the saucepan to the oven and broil until the cheese is browned, 2 to 4 minutes. Serve immediately.

OR TOP WITH:
chopped broccoli rabe (sautéed 10 to 12 minutes) + garlic + fresh mozzarella

Butternut Squash Curry with Bulgur

Prepare 1 cup uncooked bulgur according to package directions (or reheat about 3 cups cooked bulgur).

Meanwhile, heat 2 tablespoons vegetable oil in a large skillet over medium heat. Add 1 chopped shallot, ¼ cup chopped peeled fresh ginger, and 3 sliced garlic cloves, stirring occasionally, until tender, about 3 minutes.

Peel and seed 1 small butternut squash (1½ pounds) and cut it into 1-inch chunks; set aside. In a medium bowl, stir together 1 cup coconut milk, ⅓ cup smooth peanut butter, 2 tablespoons red curry paste, ½ teaspoon ground cumin, and ½ teaspoon ground cayenne pepper, and set sauce aside.

When the vegetables in the skillet are tender, add the squash, 1½ cups vegetable broth, and the reserved sauce. Cover partially, and simmer until the squash is tender, about 15 minutes. Serve the squash curry over the bulgur, sprinkled with sesame seeds and fresh mint leaves.

Serve with store-bought naan bread or cooked rice.

Mustard Greens + Paneer with Indian Spices

Heat 2 tablespoons vegetable oil in a large skillet over medium-high heat. Add 8 ounces paneer cheese, cut into 1-inch cubes, and fry until golden, 6 to 8 minutes; transfer to a plate.

A fresh farmer-type cheese; or use firm tofu

   Place ½ teaspoon garam masala, ½ teaspoon ground turmeric, and ¼ teaspoon ground cayenne pepper in the skillet, and toast until fragrant, about 30 seconds. Add coarsely chopped leaves from 1 bunch mustard greens and cook, tossing occasionally, until wilted and tender, 5 to 7 minutes. Stir in the paneer and serve with the naan or rice.

ALSO TRY:
spinach + paneer + curry powder + lemon juice

Spicy Soft Tofu with Fresh Chiles + Charred Green Beans

Heat 2 tablespoons vegetable oil in a large cast-iron or other heavy skillet over medium heat. Add 1 pound trimmed green beans, season with salt and pepper, and cook, partially covered and without stirring, until lightly charred and very tender, about 15 minutes.

Meanwhile, whisk together ¼ cup water, 2 teaspoons sugar, 2 tablespoons soy sauce, 2 teaspoons sesame oil, and 1 tablespoon cornstarch in a small bowl; set aside. Heat 2 tablespoons canola oil in a large skillet over high heat. Add 3 minced garlic cloves, 1 tablespoon minced peeled fresh ginger, chopped whites from 2 scallions (slice and reserve the greens), 3 chopped fresh hot chiles, and 1 teaspoon Szechuan peppercorns, and *or regular black peppercorns* cook, stirring, until fragrant, 2 minutes. Drain 1 package (14 ounces) soft tofu, cut it into 2-inch cubes, and gently stir it in.

Add the sauce to the skillet and cook, stirring gently, until thickened, 1 to 2 minutes. Serve the tofu over rice with the green beans and reserved scallion greens.

Fried Eggplant with Whipped Tahini Sauce, Mint + Chile

Place ½ cup flour on a rimmed plate. Lightly beat together 2 large eggs in a shallow bowl. In another shallow bowl, stir together 1 cup panko breadcrumbs, ½ teaspoon paprika, and ½ teaspoon ground cumin. Season the flour, eggs, and panko mixture with salt and pepper.

Slice 2 small eggplants into 1-inch-thick rounds. Dip them in the flour and then the egg, allowing the excess to drip off, then dredge them in the panko mixture; set aside.

Pour olive oil into a large skillet to a depth of ¼ inch and set it over medium heat. When the oil is hot, add the eggplant and cook, turning once, until it is golden brown and crispy, 6 to 8 minutes. Transfer the fried eggplant to a paper-towel-lined plate.

Meanwhile, whisk together ⅓ cup tahini, 1 tablespoon fresh lemon juice, and 2 to 4 tablespoons cold water in a small bowl until the consistency of thick yogurt. Top the eggplant with the tahini sauce, ¼ cup fresh mint leaves, and 1 chopped fresh hot chile, and serve with lemon wedges alongside.

A pinch of breadcrumbs will sizzle and begin to brown.

Baked Butter Beans in Honeyed Oregano Tomato Sauce with Feta + Pita

Preheat the oven to 425°F. Wrap 4 pita breads in foil and place them in the oven.

Heat 2 tablespoons olive oil in a large ovenproof skillet over medium-high heat. Add 1 pint cherry tomatoes, ¼ cup water, 1 tablespoon honey, ¼ teaspoon red pepper flakes, 1 crushed garlic clove, and 2 sprigs fresh oregano; cover and cook until the tomatoes begin to burst, 4 minutes. Stir in 2 cans (15 ounces each) butter beans, drained and rinsed, and transfer to the oven.

Bake the beans until the juice from the tomatoes has reduced by half, about 8 minutes. Add 4 ounces feta cheese, broken into large chunks, and bake until the feta softens, 5 minutes. Remove the beans and pita from the oven. Sprinkle the beans with fresh oregano leaves and a drizzle of olive oil before serving with the warm pita.

Burnt Caramel Pudding with Toasted Almonds

Whisk together 3 tablespoons cornstarch and 4 large egg yolks in a large heat-proof bowl, Gradually whisk in 1½ cups goat's (or cow's) milk. Set aside.

Combine 1 cup sugar, ¾ teaspoon kosher salt, and ¼ cup water in a medium saucepan, and cook, without stirring, over medium to medium-high heat until the sugar dissolves. Continue to cook, swirling the pan occasionally, until the caramel is deep amber and beginning to smoke, about 10 minutes.

Tilt the pan away from you and immediately pour in ½ cup heavy cream in a thin stream. Cook, stirring, until the caramel dissolves. *— Careful, it may splatter!*

Slowly whisk the hot caramel mixture into the egg mixture. Return the mixture to the saucepan and cook stirring constantly, over medium heat, until the first large bubble appears and the pudding thickens, 6 to 8 minutes. Remove from heat and stir in 2 tablespoons cold unsalted butter and 1 teaspoon pure vanilla extract.

Spoon the warm pudding into small glasses, and divide ¼ cup chopped dry-roasted almonds (preferably unsalted) over the top. Serve warm or chilled.

Or toast raw almonds in a small pan over medium heat for 2 to 3 minutes.

OR TOP WITH:
chopped salted peanuts + drizzle of melted dark chocolate

Peaches in Rose Syrup

Available online and in Middle Eastern markets ←

Combine 1 cup sugar, 1 cup rose water, ½ cup water, and a pinch of salt in a large skillet with a lid, and bring to a boil. Add 4 ripe peaches, halved and pitted, cut-side down and reduce the heat to low. Simmer the peaches in the syrup for about 2 minutes, then remove the saucepan from the heat, cover, and let stand to soften, 10 minutes. Serve warm or chilled.

ALSO TRY:
plums + red wine

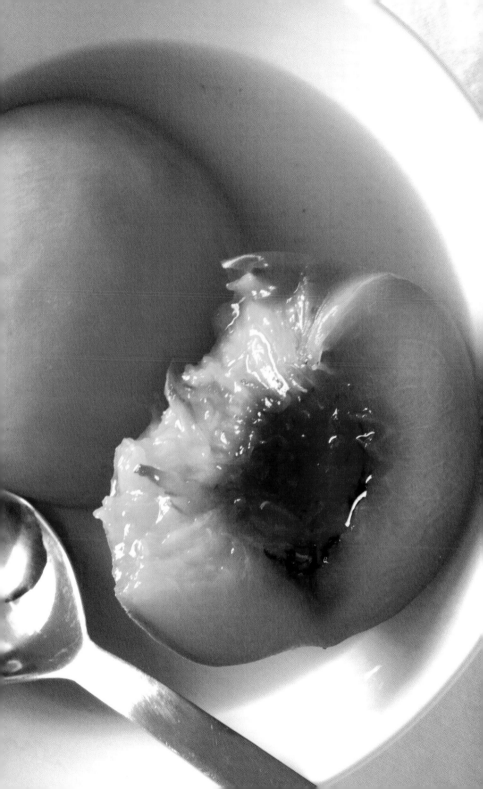

Sweetened Whipped Cream with Smashed Strawberries + Crushed Shortbread

Combine 1 cup ripe strawberries, halved; 2 tablespoons sugar; and 1 teaspoon fresh lemon juice in a medium bowl. Using your hands or a potato masher, crush the strawberries until the sugar is dissolved. Set aside for 5 minutes.

Meanwhile, in a large, clean bowl, whip 1¼ cups chilled heavy cream with an electric mixer until stiff peaks form.

Fold the strawberry mixture into the whipped cream and spoon into glasses. Divide ½ cup crushed shortbread among the glasses and serve immediately.

ALSO TRY:
whipped cream + smashed blueberries + crumbled graham crackers

Crêpes with Lemon, Molasses + Butter

Whisk together ½ cup all-purpose flour, ¼ teaspoon salt, ⅔ cup milk, 2 large eggs, 1 tablespoon melted salted butter, and 1 tablespoon dark, unsulphured molasses in a medium bowl until smooth. Lightly grease a medium nonstick skillet with a thin layer of softened salted butter and place it over medium heat.

When the skillet is hot, swirl about 2 tablespoons of the batter into the pan to create a thin pancake. Cook the crêpe, flipping it when the top is no longer wet-looking, until evenly browned on both sides, about 3 minutes total. Transfer the crêpe to a platter, folding it in half, and cover it with a clean kitchen towel. Repeat with the remaining batter (you'll have 8 to 10 crêpes).

To serve, drizzle the warm crêpes with 2 tablespoons molasses and a generous squeeze of fresh lemon juice, and dab with about 2 tablespoons salted butter.

ALSO TRY:
crêpes + honey + mascarpone cheese

Toasted Brioche with Meyer Lemon Curd + Black Peppered Berries

Whisk together 6 large egg yolks, ½ cup fresh Meyer or regular lemon juice (from about 4 lemons), and ⅔ cup sugar in a small saucepan over medium heat. Cook, stirring constantly, until the curd is thick enough to coat a spoon, 13 to 15 minutes. Stir in 3 tablespoons cold unsalted butter (it will melt).

Spread the warm lemon curd over 4 slices toasted brioche, scatter 1 cup mixed berries over top, and sprinkle with ground black pepper before serving.

Or challah

ALSO TRY:
vanilla ice cream + lemon curd + pitted cherries

French Bread, Chocolate + Red Wine

Place ½ medium baguette, warm or at room temperature, and ½ bar (about 1½ ounces) best-quality bittersweet chocolate on a serving tray. To eat, tear off pieces of bread and top each with square of chocolate. Serve with glasses of red wine.

Any red does the trick, but I like Pinot Noir or Beaujolais.

Dark Chocolate Gelato Buttermilk Milkshakes

Blend together 1 pint chocolate gelato, softened, and 1½ cups buttermilk in a blender until thick and creamy. With the motor running, slowly pour in 2 ounces melted, cooled bittersweet chocolate. Pour into four glasses and serve immediately.

This isn't technically a 20-minutes-or-less recipe—the light pudding takes time to set up—but it's so special (and easy) I had to include it.

Lemon Posset

Combine **2 cups heavy cream** and **¾ cup sugar** in a small saucepan over medium heat. Stirring constantly, bring the mixture to a boil, then stop stirring and let it boil for 3 minutes. Remove the saucepan from the heat and stir in **⅓ cup fresh lemon juice.** Let the posset cool, without stirring, for 10 minutes, then transfer it to glasses or ramekins and refrigerate, uncovered, until set, about 2 hours.

Mango Ginger Lassi

Blend together 2 cups chopped mango, ¼ cup sugar, and 1 tablespoon chopped peeled fresh ginger in a blender. With the motor running, slowly pour in 2 cups kefir and blend until combined. Transfer the lassi to a pitcher and stir in 2 cups additional kefir. Serve immediately.

A fermented milk drink; use buttermilk or plain yogurt in a pinch.

ALSO TRY:
apricot + lemon zest + buttermilk

Stay-Put Fudge Sauce

It's thick like fudge but firms up when it hits the ice cream— great for cones!

Fill a medium saucepan with water to a depth of about 1 inch and bring to a simmer over low heat. Set a metal bowl over the water (it should be big enough to rest on the edge of the pan), and add 4 tablespoons unsalted butter, cut into pieces; 2 bars (3 ounces each) semisweet chocolate, chopped; 2 bars (3 ounces each) milk chocolate, chopped; and ¼ cup evaporated milk. Stir until a few pieces of chocolate remain; remove from heat and stir until completely melted. Stir in ½ to 1 cup finely chopped pecans.

Makes 1½ cups. To store, refrigerate in an airtight container for up to 2 weeks; reheat to serve.

Ice Cream Sundaes 3 Ways

BASIC TECHNIQUE Divide 1 pint ice cream among four serving bowls. Top each with one-quarter of the sundae ingredients. Serve immediately.

Olive Oil, Sea Salt + Lemon Zest Sundae

¼ cup extra-virgin olive oil
½ teaspoon finely grated fresh lemon zest

Just before serving, sprinkle each sundae with a pinch of sea salt.

Smashed Cherries + Pistachio Sundae

½ cup shelled pistachios, toasted if desired

2 cups cherries, pitted

Crush with the bottom of a sturdy glass to remove the pits.

Bourbon-Espresso Affogato Sundae

¼ cup bourbon

½ cup hot brewed espresso

Conversion Table

Weight Conversions

US/UK	METRIC
½ oz	15 g
1 oz	30 g
1½ oz	45 g
2 oz	60 g
2½ oz	75 g
3 oz	90 g
3½ oz	100 g
4 oz	125 g
5 oz	150 g
6 oz	175 g
7 oz	200 g
8 oz	250 g
9 oz	275 g
10 oz	300 g
11 oz	325 g
12 oz	350 g
13 oz	375 g
14 oz	400 g
15 oz	450 g
1 lb	500 g

Oven Temperatures

FAHRENHEIT	GAS MARK	CELSIUS
250	½	120
275	1	140
300	2	150
325	3	160
350	4	180
375	5	190
400	6	200
425	7	220
450	8	230
475	9	240
500	10	260

Note: Reduce the temperature by 20°C (68°F) for fan-assisted ovens.

Liquid Conversions

U.S.	IMPERIAL	METRIC
2 tbs	1 fl oz	30 ml
3 tbs	1½ fl oz	45 ml
¼ cup	2 fl oz	60 ml
⅓ cup	2½ fl oz	75 ml
⅓ cup + 1 tbs	3 fl oz	90 ml
⅓ cup + 2 tbs	3½ fl oz	100 ml
½ cup	4 fl oz	125 ml
⅔ cup	5 fl oz	150 ml
¾ cup	6 fl oz	175 ml
¾ cup + 2 tbs	7 fl oz	200 ml
1 cup	8 fl oz	250 ml
1 cup + 2 tbs	9 fl oz	275 ml
1¼ cups	10 fl oz	300 ml
1⅓ cups	11 fl oz	325 ml
½ cups	12 fl oz	350 ml
1⅔ cups	13 fl oz	375 ml
1¾ cups	14 fl oz	400 ml
1¾ cups + 2 tbs	15 fl oz	450 ml
2 cups (1 pint)	16 fl oz	500 ml
2½ cups	20 fl oz (1 pint)	600 ml
3¾ cups	1½ pints	900 ml
4 cups	1¾ pints	1 liter

Approximate Equivalents

1 stick butter = 8 tbs = 4 oz = ½ cup = 115 g

1 cup all-purpose presifted flour = 4.7 oz

1 cup granulated sugar = 8 oz = 220 g

1 cup (firmly packed) brown sugar = 6 oz = 220 g to 230 g

1 cup confectioners' sugar = 4½ oz = 115 g

1 cup honey or syrup = 12 oz

1 cup grated cheese = 4 oz

1 cup dried beans = 6 oz

1 large egg = about 2 oz or about 3 tbs

1 egg yolk = about 1 tbs

1 egg white = about 2 tbs

Please note that all conversions are approximate but close enough to be useful when converting from one system to another.

Index

A

Anchovy(ies):
butter, grilled asparagus + sliced
potato salad with, 18
crushed tomato, + provolone pizza, 91
fettuccine puttanesca, 69
Apples, sautéed, + thyme, potato latkes
with, 149
Apricot, Fontina, + prosciutto
sandwiches, grilled, 57
Arugula:
+ Cheddar sandwiches, grilled, 56
grilled summer squash + haloumi
salad, 6
ground lamb + butternut squash
salad with chile-cilantro oil, 20
+ speck pizza, 90
warm cranberry bean salad with
greens + breadcrumbs, 8
Asparagus:
edamame + pan-fried tofu, simple
miso soup with, 35
+ fresh goat cheese, omelets with, 93
grilled, + sliced potato salad with
anchovy butter, 18
pasta primavera, 63
soup with dill oil, 36
Avocado, baby spinach, + Sriracha egg
sandwiches, 104

B

Bacon:
+ egg tart, Alsatian, 88
orzo risotto with pancetta +
radicchio, 73

Basil:
oil, peaches, prosciutto + mozzarella,
grilled escarole with, 4
ricotta, + pepper pizza, 91
Bean(s):
butter, baked, in honeyed oregano
tomato sauce with feta + pita, 161
choosing, for recipes, xii
cranberry, salad, warm, with greens +
breadcrumbs, 8
curried chickpeas with rice, 145
fava, mint + ricotta crostino, 38
green, charred, + fresh chiles, spicy
soft tofu with, 157
kale farinata soup with fried capers, 31
+ kale salad, warm, roasted sausage
with, 118
panzanella with green olives,
mozzarella, prosciutto + tomatoes,
14
simple miso soup with asparagus,
edamame + pan-fried tofu, 35
tomatillo huevos rancheros, 99
white, + escarole ragù with harissa
oil, 147
see also Lentil(s)
Beef:
piadini with pulled bresaola, baby
Kale + Parmesan, 82
steak with herb sauce + buttered
radishes, 106
Berries:
black peppered, + Meyer lemon curd,
toasted brioche with, 170
sweetened whipped cream with
smashed strawberries + crushed
shortbread, 166

Beverages:
  dark chocolate gelato buttermilk
    milkshakes, 174
  mango-ginger lassi, 178
Bourbon-espresso affogato sundae, 183
Bread(s):
  French, chocolate + red wine, 172
  panzanella with green olives,
    mozzarella, prosciutto + tomatoes,
    14
  pappa al pomodoro (tomato + bread
    soup), 33
  toasted brioche with Meyer lemon
    curd + black peppered berries, 170
Broccoli rabe + ricotta, pasta
  handkerchiefs with, 75
Bulgur, butternut squash curry with, 153
Burgers:
  merguez, with cucumber dressing, 48
  salmon, California-style, 50
Butter, for recipes, xii

C

Cabbage, braised green, prosciutto +
  olives, spaghetti with, 65
Caramel pudding, burnt, with toasted
  almonds, 162
Carrot-ginger soup, 37
Catfish sandwiches with radish
  rémoulade, 52
Cauliflower soup with capers + parsley,
  37
Celery root rösti with Gruyère + eggs,
  97
Cheese:
  baked eggs with greens + Cheddar,
    101
  celery root rösti with Gruyère + eggs,
    97
  Cheddar, roasted red pepper +
    balsamic egg sandwiches, 105
  croques madames Florentine, 54
  crushed tomato, anchovy + provolone
    pizza, 91
  fava, mint + ricotta crostino, 38

  goat, fresh, + asparagus, omelets
    with, 93
  goat, thyme + charred tomatoes on
    toast, 40
  grilled Cheddar + arugula
    sandwiches, 56
  grilled fontina, prosciutto + apricot
    sandwiches, 57
  grilled Havarti sandwiches with
    pepperoncini, 57
  grilled summer squash + haloumi
    salad, 6
  leek and parsley pizza with lemon +
    olive oil, 91
  mustard greens + paneer with Indian
    spices, 155
  pasta handkerchiefs with broccoli
    rabe + ricotta, 75
  piadini with pulled bresaola, balsamic
    + Parmesan, 82
  polenta with mushrooms + Taleggio,
    151
  ricotta, pepper + basil pizza, 91
  roasted haloumi, scallions + cherry
    tomatoes with couscous, 143
  spaghetti cacio e pepe, 77
  tomatillo huevos rancheros, 99
  zucchini ribbon salad with potatoes,
    ricotta salata, dill, peas + radishes,
    16
  see also Feta; Mozzarella
Cherries, smashed, + pistachio sundae,
  183
Chicken:
  cutlets, breaded, with pea salad, 126
  cutlets, grilled, with grapefruit +
    watercress salad, 124
  poached, + buttermilk dressing,
    spring green salad with, 2
  thighs, grilled, with herbed tomato
    salad, 128
Chile(s):
  cherry tomatoes, + ginger, baked fish
    with, 139
  -cilantro oil, ground lamb + butternut
    squash salad with, 20

for recipes, xiii
fresh, + charred green beans, spicy
soft tofu with, 157
fresh, + summer tomato pizza, 90
spicy mussel soup, 23
whipped tahini sauce, + mint, fried
eggplant with, 159
Chocolate:
dark, gelato buttermilk milkshakes,
174
French bread + red wine, 172
stay-put fudge sauce, 180
Cilantro-chile oil, ground lamb +
butternut squash salad with, 20
Colcannon, 122
Cornmeal:
kale farinata soup with fried capers, 31
polenta with mushrooms + Taleggio,
151
Couscous:
roasted haloumi, scallions + cherry
tomatoes with, 143
white bean + escarole ragù with
harissa oil, 147
Crêpes with lemon, molasses + butter,
168
Croques madames Florentine, 54
Cucumber(s):
dressing, merguez burgers with, 48
grilled gazpacho, 27
marinated, + feta sandwiches, 42
oregano + feta, grilled lamb chops
with, 108
Curried chickpeas with rice, 145
Curry, butternut squash, with bulgur,
153

D

Dandelion greens, Greek lemon + egg
soup with, 25
Desserts:
bourbon-espresso affogato sundae,
183
burnt caramel pudding with toasted
almonds, 162
crêpes with lemon, molasses + butter,
168
dark chocolate gelato buttermilk
milkshakes, 174
French bread, chocolate + red wine,
172
lemon posset, 176
mango-ginger lassi, 178
olive oil, sea salt + lemon zest sundae,
182
peaches in rose syrup, 164
smashed cherries + pistachio sundae,
183
stay-put fudge sauce, 180
sweetened whipped cream with
smashed strawberries + crushed
shortbread, 166
toasted brioche with Meyer lemon
curd + black peppered berries,
170
Dill oil, asparagus soup with, 36

E

Eggplant:
fried, with whipped tahini sauce, mint
+ chile, 159
grilled vegetable sandwiches with
fresh aioli, 46
+ plum tomatoes, grilled lamb kebabs
with, 110
Egg(s):
+ bacon tart, Alsatian, 88
baked, with greens + Cheddar, 101
croques madames Florentine, 54
+ Gruyère, celery root rösti with, 97
+ lemon soup, Greek, with dandelion
greens, 25
omelets with asparagus + fresh goat
cheese, 93
poached, + braised Swiss chard,
linguine with, 67
sandwiches, baby spinach, avocado +
Sriracha, 104
sandwiches, Cheddar, roasted red
pepper + balsamic, 105

sandwiches, smashed pea, watercress
+ fresh mozzarella, 105
shakshuka, 95
spaghetti frittata with spinach,
prosciutto + mozzarella, 103
tomatillo huevos rancheros, 99
Escarole:
grilled, with peaches, prosciutto,
mozzarella + basil oil, 4
+ white bean ragù with harissa oil, 147
Espresso-bourbon affogato sundae, 183

F

Fennel + tomatoes, roasted sausage
meatballs with, 120
Feta:
cucumber, + oregano, grilled lamb
chops with, 108
lemon, sesame seeds + fresh oregano,
grilled flatbread with, 86
+ marinated cucumber sandwiches,
42
+ pita, baked butter beans in honeyed
oregano tomato sauce with, 161
Fish:
baked, in packets 3 ways, 138–39
baked, with browned butter +
balsamic vinegar, 138
baked, with cherry tomatoes, chile +
ginger, 139
baked, with oranges + olives, 139
California-style salmon burgers, 50
catfish sandwiches with radish
rémoulade, 52
grilled sardines + polenta with onions
+ raisins, 136
lentil + tuna salad with kalamata
olives, 12
seared salmon with orange-rosemary
lentils, 134
see also Anchovy(ies)
French bread, chocolate + red wine, 172
Frittata, spaghetti, with spinach,
prosciutto + mozzarella, 103
Fruit. see specific fruits

G

Garlic sauce, fresh, linguine with, 71
Gazpacho, grilled, 27
Gelato, dark chocolate, buttermilk
milkshakes, 174
Ginger:
-carrot soup, 37
cherry tomatoes, + chile, baked fish
with, 139
-mango lassi, 178
Grains:
butternut squash curry with bulgur,
153
curried chickpeas with rice, 145
Greek lemon + egg soup with
dandelion greens, 25
grilled sardines + polenta with onions
+ raisins, 136
kale farinata soup with fried capers, 31
polenta with mushrooms + Taleggio,
151
shrimp + grits, 132
Grapefruit + watercress salad, grilled
chicken cutlets with, 124
Green beans, charred, + fresh chiles,
spicy soft tofu with, 157
Greens:
dandelion, Greek lemon + egg soup
with, 25
grilled chicken cutlets with grapefruit
+ watercress salad, 124
grilled escarole with peaches,
prosciutto, mozzarella + basil oil, 4
linguine with braised Swiss chard +
poached egg, 67
mustard, + paneer with Indian spices,
155
orzo risotto with pancetta +
radicchio, 73
pasta primavera, 63
radish, watercress + butter
sandwiches, 44
salad, buying and storing, xii
seared pork chops with blood
orange, mint + wilted radicchio, 116

smashed pea, watercress + fresh
  mozzarella egg sandwiches, 105
spaghetti with ramps + breadcrumbs,
  59
spring green salad with poached
  chicken + buttermilk dressing, 2
white bean + escarole ragù with
  harissa oil, 147
see also Arugula; Escarole; Kale;
  Mustard Greens; Spinach
Grits + shrimp, 132

H, I

Ham:
  colcannon, 122
  see also Pancetta; Prosciutto; Speck
Harissa oil, white bean + escarole ragù
  with, 147
Ice cream sundaes 3 ways, 182–83

K

Kale:
  baked eggs with greens + Cheddar,
    101
  + bean salad, warm, roasted sausage
    with, 118
  colcannon, 122
  farinata soup with fried capers, 31
  pulled bresaola, baby kale +
    Parmesan, piadini with, 82

L

Lamb:
  chops, grilled, with cucumber,
    oregano + feta, 108
  ground, + butternut squash salad
    with chile-cilantro oil, 20
  kebabs, grilled, with eggplant + plum
    tomatoes, 110
  merguez burgers with cucumber
    dressing, 48
Latkes, potato, with sautéed apples +
  thyme, 149

Leek and parsley pizza with lemon +
  olive oil, 91
Lemon:
  + cream, mussels + sweet sausage
    with, 141
  + egg soup, Greek, with dandelion
    greens, 25
  Meyer, curd + black peppered berries,
    toasted brioche with, 170
  molasses, + butter, crêpes with, 168
  posset, 176
  zest, olive oil, + sea salt sundae, 182
Lentil(s):
  orange-rosemary, seared salmon
    with, 134
  red, soup with browned spice butter,
    29
  + tuna salad with kalamata olives, 12
  with turkey sausage + fried sage,
    130

M

Mango-ginger lassi, 178
Meat. *see* Beef; Lamb; Pork
Meatballs, roasted sausage, with fennel
  + tomatoes, 120
Merguez burgers with cucumber
  dressing, 48
Milkshakes, dark chocolate gelato
  buttermilk, 174
Mint:
  blood orange, + wilted radicchio,
    seared pork chops with, 116
  fava, + ricotta crostino, 38
  whipped tahini sauce, + chile, fried
    eggplant with, 159
Miso soup, simple, with asparagus,
  edamame + pan-fried tofu, 35
Molasses, lemon + butter, crêpes with,
  168
Mozzarella:
  fresh, smashed pea + watercress egg
    sandwiches, 105
  fresh, + spicy zucchini marinara,
    spaghetti with, 61

green olives, prosciutto + tomatoes,
panzanella with, 14

grilled turkey sausage + pepper
pizza, 78

peaches, prosciutto + basil oil, grilled
escarole with, 4

pesto, + salami, cast-iron pan pizza
with, 84

speck + arugula pizza, 90

spinach, + prosciutto, spaghetti
frittata with, 103

summer tomato + fresh chile pizza,
90

Mushrooms:
pasta primavera, 63
+ Taleggio, polenta with, 151

Mussel(s):
+ fresh chorizo with parsley +
peppers, 141
pizza bianco, 80
+ sausage in mustard-beer broth, 140
soup, spicy, 23
+ sweet sausage with lemon + cream,
141

Mustard greens + paneer with Indian
spices, 155

N

Noodles. *see* Soba

Nuts:
burnt caramel pudding with toasted
almonds, 162
roasted pork tenderloin with Seckel
pears + pistachios, 114
smashed cherries + pistachio sundae,
183

O

Oil, for recipes, xi

Olive oil, sea salt + lemon zest sundae,
182

Olives:
braised green cabbage, + prosciutto,
spaghetti with, 65

fettuccine puttanesca, 69

green, mozzarella, prosciutto +
tomatoes, panzanella with, 14

kalamata, lentil + tuna salad with, 12

+ oranges, baked fish with, 139

Omelets with asparagus + fresh goat
cheese, 93

Onion(s):
+ peaches, grilled, sage-rubbed pork
chops with, 112
+ raisins, grilled sardines + polenta
with, 136
three, pizza, 91

Orange(s):
blood orange, mint + wilted radicchio,
seared pork chops with, 116
+ olives, baked fish with, 139
-rosemary lentils, seared salmon with,
134

P

Pancetta + radicchio, orzo risotto with,
73

Panzanella with green olives, mozzarella,
prosciutto + tomatoes, 14

Pappa al pomodoro (tomato + bread
soup), 33

Pasta:
fettuccine puttanesca, 69
linguine with braised Swiss chard +
poached egg, 67
linguine with fresh garlic sauce, 71
matching shapes with sauces, xii
orzo risotto with pancetta +
radicchio, 73
pasta handkerchiefs with broccoli
rabe + ricotta, 75
primavera, 63
spaghetti cacio e pepe, 77
spaghetti frittata with spinach,
prosciutto + mozzarella, 103
spaghetti with braised green
cabbage, prosciutto + olives, 65
spaghetti with ramps + breadcrumbs,
59

spaghetti with spicy zucchini
marinara + fresh mozzarella, 61
see also Couscous; Soba
Peaches:
+ onions, grilled, sage-rubbed pork
chops with, 112
prosciutto, mozzarella + basil oil,
grilled escarole with, 4
in rose syrup, 164
Pears, Seckel, + pistachios, roasted pork
tenderloin with, 114
Pea(s):
pasta primavera, 63
potatoes, ricotta salata, dill +
radishes, zucchini ribbon salad
with, 16
salad, breaded chicken cutlets with,
126
smashed, watercress + fresh
mozzarella egg sandwiches, 105
Pepper, black, + cheese spaghetti, 77
Pepper(s):
grilled gazpacho, 27
grilled Havarti sandwiches with
pepperoncini, 57
grilled vegetable sandwiches with
fresh aioli, 46
+ parsley, mussels + fresh chorizo
with, 141
ricotta, + basil pizza, 91
roasted red, Cheddar + balsamic egg
sandwiches, 105
shrimp + grits, 132
+ turkey sausage pizza, grilled, 78
see also Chile(s)
Pesto, mozzarella + salami, cast-iron
pan pizza with, 84
Pizza:
Alsatian bacon + egg tart, 88
cast-iron pan, with pesto, mozzarella
+ salami, 84
crushed tomato, anchovy +
provolone, 91
grilled flatbread with feta, lemon,
sesame seeds + fresh oregano,
86

grilled turkey sausage + pepper, 78
leek and parsley, with lemon + olive
oil, 91
mussels, bianco, 80
piadini with pulled bresaola, baby
kale + Parmesan, 82
ricotta, pepper + basil, 91
speck + arugula, 90
summer tomato + fresh chile, 90
three onion, 91
Polenta:
with mushrooms + Taleggio, 151
+ sardines, grilled, with onions +
raisins, 136
Pork:
cast-iron pan pizza with pesto,
mozzarella + salami, 84
chops, sage-rubbed, with grilled
peaches + onions, 112
chops, seared, with blood orange,
mint + wilted radicchio, 116
mussels + fresh chorizo with parsley
+ peppers, 141
mussels + sausage in mustard-beer
broth, 140
mussels + sweet sausage with lemon
+ cream, 141
roasted sausage meatballs with
fennel + tomatoes, 120
roasted sausage with warm bean +
kale salad, 118
speck + arugula pizza, 90
tenderloin, roasted, with Seckel pears
+ pistachios, 114
see also Bacon; Ham; Pancetta;
Prosciutto; Speck
Potato(es):
celery root rösti with Gruyère + eggs,
97
colcannon, 122
latkes with sautéed apples + thyme,
149
ricotta salata, dill, peas + radishes,
zucchini ribbon salad with, 16
sliced, + grilled asparagus salad with
anchovy butter, 18

Poultry. *see* Chicken; Turkey sausage
Prosciutto:
    braised green cabbage, + olives,
        spaghetti with, 65
    croques madames Florentine, 54
    fontina, + apricot sandwiches, grilled,
        57
    green olives, mozzarella + tomatoes,
        panzanella with, 14
    peaches, mozzarella + basil oil, grilled
        escarole with, 4
    spinach, + mozzarella, spaghetti
        frittata with, 103
Pudding, burnt caramel, with toasted
    almonds, 162

Radicchio:
    + pancetta, orzo risotto with, 73
    wilted, blood orange + mint, seared
        pork chops with, 116
Radish(es):
    buttered, + herb sauce, steak with, 106
    rémoulade, catfish sandwiches with,
        52
    watercress + butter sandwiches, 44
Raisins + onions, grilled sardines +
    polenta with, 136
Ramps + breadcrumbs, spaghetti
    with, 59
Recipes:
    beans for, xii
    butter for, xii
    buying pantry items for, xiii
    chiles for, xii
    gathering ingredients for, x–xi
    oils and vinegars for, xi
    pasta for, xii
    reading through, x–xi
    seasonal produce for, xi
    substituting ingredients, xi–xii
Rice:
    curried chickpeas with, 145
    Greek lemon + egg soup with
        dandelion greens, 25

Risotto, orzo, with pancetta + radicchio,
    73
Rose syrup, peaches in, 164
Rösti, celery root, with Gruyère + eggs,
    97

Sage:
    fried, + turkey sausage, lentils with,
        130
    -rubbed pork chops with grilled
        peaches + onions, 112
Salad dressings:
    buttermilk, 2
    favorite combinations, xii
    fresh aioli, 46
    simple, preparing, xii–xiii
Salads:
    bean + kale, warm, roasted sausage
        with, 118
    cold spicy soba + spinach, with
        shrimp, 10
    grapefruit + watercress, grilled
        chicken cutlets with, 124
    grilled asparagus + sliced potato,
        with anchovy butter, 18
    grilled escarole with peaches,
        prosciutto, mozzarella + basil oil, 4
    grilled summer squash + haloumi, 6
    ground lamb + butternut squash, with
        chile-cilantro oil, 20
    lentil + tuna, with kalamata olives, 12
    panzanella with green olives,
        mozzarella, prosciutto + tomatoes,
        14
    pea, breaded chicken cutlets with, 126
    spring green, with poached chicken +
        buttermilk dressing, 2
    tomato, herbed, grilled chicken thighs
        with, 128
    warm cranberry bean, with greens +
        breadcrumbs, 8
    zucchini ribbon, with potatoes,
        ricotta salata, dill, peas + radishes,
        16